The Poetry of Sex

The Poetry of Sex

EDITED BY SOPHIE HANNAH

VIKING
an imprint of
PENGUIN BOOKS

VIKING

Published by the Penguin Group
Penguin Books Ltd, 80 Strand, London WC2R 0RL, England
Penguin Group (USA) Inc., 375 Hudson Street, New York, New York 10014, USA
Penguin Group (Canada), 90 Eglinton Avenue East, Suite 700, Toronto, Ontario, Canada M4P 2Y3
(a division of Pearson Penguin Canada Inc.)
Penguin Ireland, 25 St Stephen's Green, Dublin 2, Ireland (a division of Penguin Books Ltd)
Penguin Group (Australia), 707 Collins Street, Melbourne, Victoria 3008, Australia
(a division of Pearson Australia Group Pty Ltd)
Penguin Books India Pvt Ltd, 11 Community Centre, Panchsheel Park, New Delhi – 110 017, India
Penguin Group (NZ), 67 Apollo Drive, Rosedale, Auckland 0632, New Zealand
(a division of Pearson New Zealand Ltd)
Penguin Books (South Africa) (Pty) Ltd, Block D, Rosebank Office Park,
181 Jan Smuts Avenue, Parktown North, Gauteng 2193, South Africa

Penguin Books Ltd, Registered Offices: 80 Strand, London WC2R 0RL, England

www.penguin.com

First published 2014
001

This selection copyright © Sophie Hannah, 2014
Introduction copyright © Sophie Hannah, 2014

The moral right of the author has been asserted

The acknowledgements that appear on p. 203 constitute an extension of this copyright page.

Every effort has been made to trace copyright holders and to obtain their permission for the use of
copyright material. The publisher apologizes for any errors or omissions and would be grateful
to be notified of any corrections that should be incorporated in future editions of this book.

Set in 10/14pt Monotype Sabon
Typeset by Jouve (UK), Milton Keynes
Printed in Great Britain by Clays Ltd, St Ives plc

A CIP catalogue record for this book is available from the British Library

ISBN: 978-0-670-92183-6

www.greenpenguin.co.uk

Penguin Books is committed to a sustainable
future for our business, our readers and our planet.
This book is made from Forest Stewardship
Council™ certified paper.

Contents

3 'A night picked from a hundred and one'

4 'All our states united'

5 'But your wife said she'

6 'What's in it for me?'

7 'Oh right. You people don't remove that bit'

8 'God, to be wanted once more'

Introduction

There are two poems in this book about the actor Daniel Craig, and none about any other Hollywood star. While the situation with regard to rock and pop legends is a little (though not much) more equitable, with Mick Jagger and David Cassidy cropping up in one poem each, it is impossible to deny that, on the actor front, this anthology is heavily biased in favour of Daniel Craig over and above all others.

I draw readers' attention to this feature of the book because I wouldn't want anyone to imagine I'm unaware of it. Editors of poetry anthologies, like the judges of literary prizes, are often criticized for perceived imbalances of this sort. As a committed positive-discrimination enthusiast, when I saw that a weighting in favour of Daniel Craig was a risk, I tried to redress the balance by introducing an All-Tom-Cruise shortlisting policy, but then had to abandon it when I found not a single poem about Tom Cruise, which suggests that the teaching of creative writing has been woefully inadequate for the last twenty years, or however long it is since *Risky Business* came out.

All might be fair in love and war (though in fact it isn't), but all is certainly not fair in sex. Nevertheless, Daniel Craig stranglehold notwithstanding, there is much diversity in this anthology – diversity of writers, of subject matter and of approach. I am happy to report that the two poems about Daniel Craig couldn't be more different from one another. One, by a male author, has its narrator gazing lustfully at a photograph of Craig when he ought to be working. The lust is enthusiastic and uncomplicated. The other Craig poem, by a woman, deals with the problems and potential life wreckage associated with sleeping with the actor, even though the narrator doesn't even like him and therefore has no desire to do so – or so she says.

It would be a mistake to conclude from this exhaustive study of two poems about Daniel Craig that women and men have radically different approaches to sex and that one is more straightforwardly physical than the other. If this book suggests any kind of generalizable truth, it is surely that each writer's experiences, psychological approach to those experiences and choice of words in expressing him- or herself are unique. Some female poets in this anthology have adopted what might be seen as a traditionally male attitude to sex, at least for as long as it takes to complete a sonnet, and could reasonably claim dual citizenship of Mars and Venus. One of my favourites included here, Edna St Vincent Millay's 'I, being born a woman and distressed', has a narrator who wishes to make it clear in advance that, once the carnal frolics are concluded, she will no longer have any use for her sexual partner; she wants his body but has no interest in his mind.

Outrageous, you might say, particularly if you were a close friend of the man in question. Indeed, if one wanted to take umbrage on behalf of ill-treated sexual partners, there are many hapless victims of poets to be found among these pages, as well as authors and narrators (and authors posing as fictional narrators, as a convenient relationship-saving device), who have been exploited and crushed by cads, the emotionally illiterate, the pathologically narcissistic and the infuriatingly married of both sexes. There are poems here that might seem misandrist or misogynist – Irving Layton's 'Bicycle Pump', for example, or Fleur Adcock's 'Madmen' – which I have included because I am more interested in the 'Is' of sex than the 'Should'. We all make sexist generalizations from time to time – often after sleeping with someone whom we perceive as typifying his or her gender. 'Men!' we cry, or 'Women!' We forget to qualify our derision with the prefix 'Some'; sexual disillusionment and a sense of proportion are largely incompatible.

There are poems in this anthology written specifically to encourage people into bed and urge them not to take too long about it – Marvell's 'To His Coy Mistress' being one brilliant example, and Wendy Cope's 'Message' another. There are poems that take a cheerful and cavalier approach to sexual behaviour that many would regard as immoral, poems about fantasizing in the direction of one lover while being in bed with another, about continuing to use a partner's body for low-level gratification when you know the relationship is over but they don't. There is a poem about getting a quick blow job in a car and then making a run for it, a poem celebrating illicit sex with colleagues in the office on the grounds that it makes the daily routine of 'wives and work' more bearable. Balancing out all of the above are the many poems about wholesome, committed, sanctioned sex that breaks no rules at all.

There was absolutely no moral weighting in the selection I made. To make this clear, I chose to name each chapter of the anthology after a line from one of the poems it contains, rather than use titles such as 'Married Sex (Holding Society Together)' and 'Adultery (Poems by Slags and Home-wreckers)'; I liked the idea of the poets being represented in their own words not only in the poems they have written but even when it came to naming the section of this book in which they would eventually find themselves. There is something dangerous about trying to define another person's sexual experience, and what might be seen externally as coming under the heading 'Adultery' could well feel more like 'Life Support' or 'My One Chance of Happiness' from the inside. It is hard to define without moralizing, and the constant attempts by many to force sex and morality together – an ineptly arranged marriage of two strangers, bound to end in disaster – often leads to absurdity. As I write this introduction, David Cameron is trying very hard to ban pornography that involves simulated rape scenes between consenting adults, even though many vocal intelligent women are waving copies of Nancy Friday's *My Secret Garden* in the air and trying to tell their prime minister that, no, they do not wish to be raped, but that, yes, they do have rape fantasies, which are an entirely different thing and should not be banned or judged. It is possible that, by the time this anthology is published, the only sexual fantasies still legal in the UK will be those that feature Ed Miliband in conversation with a group of intersectionalist feminists who check their privilege every thirty seconds.

Meanwhile, in New York, married mayoral candidate Anthony Weiner is busy being solemn and contrite at press conferences after being caught 'sexting' a woman who is not his wife, attaching pictures of his private parts and calling himself 'Carlos Danger' (which imaginative and rather sweet alias will, I hope, win him at least a few votes – particularly when one considers that Carlos Danger is an anagram of Roger Scandal, and that Roger Scandal would make a great pseudonym for a poet writing about sex).

Some, though not many, of the poems in this anthology are published under pseudonyms. Auden's brilliant poem 'The Platonic Blow' was first published under another name because of its graphic portrayal of homosexual fellatio. Nowadays, fewer readers would be shocked by that, but when it comes to sex, however far societal norms progress in the direction of enlightened thinking, people will always have something to hide. Many won't be quite sure why they need to keep their true sexual selves hidden, only that they must. For most of us, our sexual desires pose questions we cannot answer. C. H. Sisson puts it brilliantly in his poem 'I Who Am', one of my absolute favourites in this collection, so I will give the last word of this introduction to him, and hope that, wherever he is, he won't be too shocked by his role as frontman of what I hope will be the raunchiest poetry anthology of the year:

So ask the body. It alone
Knows all you know, and it imparts
Little enough of what is known
To what we call our minds and hearts.

So fumbling bodies try to make
Friendship and love as best they can:
None ever was without mistake
And lies by woman and by man.

Man lies by woman, woman lies
By man, and in a common bed.
Where is the rule which truly tries
What is done there by what is said?

I

'So ask the body'

Saturday Morning

Hugo Williams

Everyone who made love the night before
was walking around with flashing red lights
on top of their heads – a white-haired old gentleman,
a red-faced schoolboy, a pregnant woman
who smiled at me from across the street
and gave a little secret shrug,
as if the flashing red light on her head
was a small price to pay for what she knew.

The Plague

Caroline Bird

It takes more than pants and zips
to hide my cunt, it yells in its sleep,
the town is bucking, villagers are pillaging each other.
The bodies pile up, threesomes become foursomes,
the priest fucked a firework, a second coming,
a third, it's a plague, seven dwarves in one bed,
the policemen have permanent erections,
no one has any blood in their heads,
the vet does curious things to a horse,
a mattress outside every bank,
there's no point trying to read a book
not unless you take it from behind.
Someone fetch a bucket, a bible, a plug,
a hook to hang these fidgeting frocks,
even that crippled tortoise looks sexy,
my leg has burnt a hole in my trousers.

The Elephant is Slow to Mate

D. H. Lawrence

The elephant, the huge old beast,
   is slow to mate;
he finds a female, they show no haste
   they wait

for the sympathy in their vast shy hearts
   slowly, slowly to rouse
as they loiter along the river-beds
   and drink and browse

and dash in panic through the brake
   of forest with the herd,
and sleep in massive silence, and wake
   together, without a word.

So slowly the great hot elephant hearts
   grow full of desire,
and the great beasts mate in secret at last,
   hiding their fire.

Oldest they are and the wisest of beasts
   so they know at last
how to wait for the loneliest of feasts
   for the full repast.

They do not snatch, they do not tear;
   their massive blood
moves as the moon-tides, near, more near
   till they touch in flood.

On the Happy Corydon and Phyllis

Sir Charles Sedley

Young Corydon and Phyllis
Sat in a lovely grove,
Contriving crowns of lilies,
Repeating toys of love,
And something else, but what I dare not name.

But as they were a-playing,
She ogled so the swain,
It saved her plainly saying,
'Let's kiss to ease our pain,
And something else, but what I dare not name.'

A thousand times he kissed her,
Laying her on the green;
But as he further pressed her
A pretty leg was seen,
And something else, but what I dare not name.

So many beauties viewing,
His ardour still increased,
And greater joys pursuing,
He wandered o'er her breast,
And something else, but what I dare not name.

A last effort she trying
His passion to withstand,
Cried, but 'twas faintly crying,
'Pray take away your hand,
And something else, but what I dare not name.'

Young Corydon, grown bolder,
The minutes would improve,
'This is the time,' he told her,
'To show you how I love,
And something else, but what I dare not name.'

The nymph seemed almost dying,
Dissolved in amorous heat,
She kissed, and told him sighing,
'My dear, your love is great,
And something else, but what I dare not name.'

But Phyllis did recover,
Much sooner than the swain,
She blushing asked her lover,
'Shall we not kiss again,
And something else, but what I dare not name?'

Thus love his revels keeping,
Till nature at a stand,
From talk they fell to sleeping
Holding each other's hand
And something else, but what I dare not name.

No Platonic Love

William Cartwright

Tell me no more of minds embracing minds,
And hearts exchang'd for hearts;
That spirits spirits meet, as winds do winds,
And mix their subt'lest parts;
That two unbodied essences may kiss,
And then like Angels, twist and feel one Bliss.

I was that silly thing that once was wrought
To practise this thin love;
I climb'd from sex to soul, from soul to thought;
But thinking there to move,
Headlong I rolled from thought to soul, and then
From soul I lighted at the sex again.

As some strict down-looked men pretend to fast,
Who yet in closets eat;
So lovers who profess they spirits taste,
Feed yet on grosser meat;
I know they boast they souls to souls convey,
Howe'r they meet, the body is the way.

Come, I will undeceive thee, they that tread
Those vain aerial ways
Are like young heirs and alchemists misled
To waste their wealth and days,
For searching thus to be for ever rich,
They only find a med'cine for the itch.

I Who Am

C. H. Sisson

I who am and you who are –
If we are, as we suppose –
None the less are very far
From knowing what each other knows.

Even the curl of that curled leaf
Is not the same for both our eyes,
Much less a hope, much less a grief,
A memory, or a surmise.

Much less the whole that makes the Is
Of any living creature. I
May utter perfect sentences
And so may you, who make reply,

But these toy structures are no more
Than any rule held in the hand,
And what your words, or mine, are for
Is not a thing we understand,

So ask the body. It alone
Knows all you know, and it imparts
Little enough of what is known
To what we call our minds and hearts.

So fumbling bodies try to make
Friendship and love as best they can:
None ever was without mistake
And lies by woman and by man.

Man lies by woman, woman lies
By man, and in a common bed.
Where is the rule which truly tries
What is done there by what is said?

Leda and the Swan

W. B. Yeats

A sudden blow: the great wings beating still
Above the staggering girl, her thighs caressed
By the dark webs, her nape caught in his bill,
He holds her helpless breast upon his breast.

How can those terrified vague fingers push
The feathered glory from her loosening thighs?
And how can body, laid in that white rush,
But feel the strange heart beating where it lies?

A shudder in the loins engenders there
The broken wall, the burning roof and tower
And Agamemnon dead.
                    Being so caught up,
So mastered by the brute blood of the air,
Did she put on his knowledge with his power
Before the indifferent beak could let her drop?

'I, being born a woman and distressed'

Edna St Vincent Millay

I, being born a woman and distressed
By all the needs and notions of my kind,
Am urged by your propinquity to find
Your person fair, and feel a certain zest
To bear your body's weight upon my breast:
So subtly is the fume of life designed,
To clarify the pulse and cloud the mind,
And leave me once again undone, possessed.
Think not for this, however, the poor treason
Of my stout blood against my staggering brain,
I shall remember you with love, or season
My scorn with pity, – let me make it plain:
I find this frenzy insufficient reason
For conversation when we meet again.

And

Alison Brackenbury

Sex is like Criccieth. You thought it would be
a tumble of houses into a pure sea
and so it must have been, in eighteen-ten.
The ranks of boarding houses marched up then.
They linger, plastic curtains at their doors,
or, still more oddly, blonde ungainly statues.
The traffic swills along the single street
and floods the ears, until our feet
turn down towards the only shop for chips,
to shuffling queues, until sun slips
behind the Castle, which must be, by luck,
one of the few a Welsh prince ever took.
Or in the café, smoked with fat, you wait.
Will dolphins strike the sea's skin? They do not.

And yet, a giant sun nobody has told
of long decline, beats the rough sea to gold.
The Castle rears up with its tattered flag,
hand laces hand, away from valleys' slag.
And through the night, the long sea's dolphined breath
whispers into your warm ear, 'Criccieth'.

I Sing the Body Electric

Walt Whitman

1

I sing the body electric,
The armies of those I love engirth me and I engirth them,
They will not let me off till I go with them, respond to them,
And discorrupt them, and charge them full with the charge of
  the soul.

Was it doubted that those who corrupt their own bodies conceal
  themselves?
And if those who defile the living are as bad as they who defile the
  dead?
And if the body does not do fully as much as the soul?
And if the body were not the soul, what is the soul?

2

The love of the body of man or woman balks account, the body itself
  balks account,
That of the male is perfect, and that of the female is perfect.

The expression of the face balks account,
But the expression of a well-made man appears not only in his face,
It is in his limbs and joints also, it is curiously in the joints of his
  hips and wrists,
It is in his walk, the carriage of his neck, the flex of his waist
  and knees, dress does not hide him,

The strong sweet quality he has strikes through the cotton and
    broadcloth,
To see him pass conveys as much as the best poem, perhaps more,
You linger to see his back, and the back of his neck and
    shoulder-side.

The sprawl and fulness of babes, the bosoms and heads of
    women, the folds of their dress, their style as we pass in the
    street, the contour of their shape downwards,
The swimmer naked in the swimming-bath, seen as he swims
    through the transparent green-shine, or lies with his face
    up and rolls silently to and from the heave of the water,
The bending forward and backward of rowers in row-boats, the
    horse-man in his saddle,
Girls, mothers, house-keepers, in all their performances,
The group of laborers seated at noon-time with their open
    dinner-kettles, and their wives waiting,
The female soothing a child, the farmer's daughter in the garden or
    cow-yard,
The young fellow hoeing corn, the sleigh-driver driving his six
    horses through the crowd,
The wrestle of wrestlers, two apprentice-boys, quite grown, lusty,
    good-natured, native-born, out on the vacant lot at sundown
    after work,
The coats and caps thrown down, the embrace of love and
    resistance,
The upper-hold and under-hold, the hair rumpled over and
    blinding the eyes;
The march of firemen in their own costumes, the play of masculine
    muscle through clean-setting trowsers and waist-straps,
The slow return from the fire, the pause when the bell strikes
    suddenly again, and the listening on the alert,

The natural, perfect, varied attitudes, the bent head, the curv'd
    neck and the counting;
Such-like I love – I loosen myself, pass freely, am at the mother's
    breast with the little child,
Swim with the swimmers, wrestle with wrestlers, march in line with
    the firemen, and pause, listen, count.

3

I knew a man, a common farmer, the father of five sons,
And in them the fathers of sons, and in them the fathers of sons.

This man was of wonderful vigor, calmness, beauty of person,
The shape of his head, the pale yellow and white of his hair and
    beard, the immeasurable meaning of his black eyes, the richness
    and breadth of his manners,
These I used to go and visit him to see, he was wise also,
He was six feet tall, he was over eighty years old, his sons were
    massive, clean, bearded, tan-faced, handsome,
They and his daughters loved him, all who saw him loved him,
They did not love him by allowance, they loved him with personal
    love,
He drank water only, the blood show'd like scarlet through the
    clear-brown skin of his face,
He was a frequent gunner and fisher, he sail'd his boat himself, he
    had a fine one presented to him by a ship-joiner, he had
    fowling-pieces presented to him by men that loved him,
When he went with his five sons and many grand-sons to hunt or fish,
    you would pick him out as the most beautiful and vigorous of
    the gang,
You would wish long and long to be with him, you would wish to sit
    by him in the boat that you and he might touch each other.

4

I have perceiv'd that to be with those I like is enough,
To stop in company with the rest at evening is enough,
To be surrounded by beautiful, curious, breathing, laughing flesh is
  enough,
To pass among them or touch any one, or rest my arm ever so
  lightly round his or her neck for a moment, what is this then?
I do not ask any more delight, I swim in it as in a sea.

There is something in staying close to men and women and
  looking on them, and in the contact and odor of them, that
  pleases the soul well,
All things please the soul, but these please the soul well.

5

This is the female form,
A divine nimbus exhales from it from head to foot,
It attracts with fierce undeniable attraction,
I am drawn by its breath as if I were no more than a helpless
  vapor, all falls aside but myself and it,
Books, art, religion, time, the visible and solid earth, and what
  was expected of heaven or fear'd of hell, are now consumed,
Mad filaments, ungovernable shoots play out of it, the response
  likewise ungovernable,
Hair, bosom, hips, bend of legs, negligent falling hands all
  diffused, mine too diffused,
Ebb stung by the flow and flow stung by the ebb, love-flesh swelling
  and deliciously aching,
Limitless limpid jets of love hot and enormous, quivering jelly of
  love, white-blow and delirious nice,

Bridegroom night of love working surely and softly into the
    prostrate dawn,
Undulating into the willing and yielding day,
Lost in the cleave of the clasping and sweet-flesh'd day.

This the nucleus – after the child is born of woman, man is born
    of woman,
This the bath of birth, this the merge of small and large, and the
    outlet again.

Be not ashamed women, your privilege encloses the rest, and is the
    exit of the rest,
You are the gates of the body, and you are the gates of the soul.

The female contains all qualities and tempers them,
She is in her place and moves with perfect balance,
She is all things duly veil'd, she is both passive and active,
She is to conceive daughters as well as sons, and sons as well as
    daughters.

As I see my soul reflected in Nature,
As I see through a mist, One with inexpressible completeness,
    sanity, beauty,
See the bent head and arms folded over the breast, the Female
    I see.

6

The male is not less the soul nor more, he too is in his place,
He too is all qualities, he is action and power,
The flush of the known universe is in him,
Scorn becomes him well, and appetite and defiance become him well,
The wildest largest passions, bliss that is utmost, sorrow that is
    utmost become him well, pride is for him,

The full-spread pride of man is calming and excellent to the soul,
Knowledge becomes him, he likes it always, he brings every
    thing to the test of himself,
Whatever the survey, whatever the sea and the sail he strikes
    soundings at last only here,
(Where else does he strike soundings except here?)

The man's body is sacred and the woman's body is sacred,
No matter who it is, it is sacred – is it the meanest one in the
    laborers' gang?
Is it one of the dull-faced immigrants just landed on the wharf?
Each belongs here or anywhere just as much as the well-off, just as
    much as you,
Each has his or her place in the procession.

(All is a procession,
The universe is a procession with measured and perfect motion.)

Do you know so much yourself that you call the meanest
    ignorant?
Do you suppose you have a right to a good sight, and he or
    she has no right to a sight?
Do you think matter has cohered together from its diffuse float, and
    the soil is on the surface, and water runs and vegetation
    sprouts,
For you only, and not for him and her?

7

A man's body at auction,
(For before the war I often go to the slave-mart and watch the
    sale,)
I help the auctioneer, the sloven does not half know his business.

*

Gentlemen look on this wonder,
Whatever the bids of the bidders they cannot be high enough
    for it,
For it the globe lay preparing quintillions of years without one
    animal or plant,
For it the revolving cycles truly and steadily roll'd.

In this head the all-baffling brain,
In it and below it the makings of heroes.

Examine these limbs, red, black, or white, they are cunning in
    tendon and nerve,
They shall be stript that you may see them.
Exquisite senses, life-lit eyes, pluck, volition,
Flakes of breast-muscle, pliant backbone and neck, flesh not
    flabby, good-sized arms and legs,
And wonders within there yet.

Within there runs blood,
The same old blood! the same red-running blood!
There swells and jets a heart, there all passions, desires, reachings,
    aspirations,
(Do you think they are not there because they are not express'd in
    parlors and lecture-rooms?)

This is not only one man, this the father of those who shall be
    fathers in their turns,
In him the start of populous states and rich republics,
Of him countless immortal lives with countless embodiments and
    enjoyments.

*

How do you know who shall come from the offspring of his
 offspring through the centuries?
(Who might you find you have come from yourself, if you could
 trace back through the centuries?)

8

A woman's body at auction,
She too is not only herself, she is the teeming mother of
 mothers,
She is the bearer of them that shall grow and be mates to the
 mothers.

Have you ever loved the body of a woman?
Have you ever loved the body of a man?
Do you not see that these are exactly the same to all in all
 nations and times all over the earth?

If any thing is sacred the human body is sacred,
And the glory and sweet of a man is the token of manhood
 untainted,
And in man or woman a clean, strong, firm-fibred body, is more
 beautiful
 than the most beautiful face.
Have you seen the fool that corrupted his own live body? or
 the fool that corrupted her own live body?
For they do not conceal themselves, and cannot conceal
 themselves.

9

O my body! I dare not desert the likes of you in other men and
 women, nor the likes of the parts of you,

I believe the likes of you are to stand or fall with the likes of the
    soul, (and that they are the soul,)
I believe the likes of you shall stand or fall with my poems, and
    that they are my poems,
Man's, woman's, child's, youth's, wife's, husband's, mother's,
    father's, young man's, young woman's poems,
Head, neck, hair, ears, drop and tympan of the ears,
Eyes, eye-fringes, iris of the eye, eyebrows, and the waking or
    sleeping of the lids,
Mouth, tongue, lips, teeth, roof of the mouth, jaws, and the
    jaw-hinges,
Nose, nostrils of the nose, and the partition,
Cheeks, temples, forehead, chin, throat, back of the neck,
    neck-slue,
Strong shoulders, manly beard, scapula, hind-shoulders, and the
    ample side-round of the chest,
Upper-arm, armpit, elbow-socket, lower-arm, arm-sinews,
    arm-bones,
Wrist and wrist-joints, hand, palm, knuckles, thumb, forefinger,
    finger-joints, finger-nails,
Broad breast-front, curling hair of the breast, breast-bone,
    breast-side,
Ribs, belly, backbone, joints of the backbone,
Hips, hip-sockets, hip-strength, inward and outward round,
    man-balls, man-root,
Strong set of thighs, well carrying the trunk above,
Leg-fibres, knee, knee-pan, upper-leg, under-leg,
Ankles, instep, foot-ball, toes, toe-joints, the heel;
All attitudes, all the shapeliness, all the belongings of my or
    your body or of any one's body, male or female,
The lung-sponges, the stomach-sac, the bowels sweet and clean,
The brain in its folds inside the skull-frame,
Sympathies, heart-valves, palate-valves, sexuality, maternity,

Womanhood, and all that is a woman, and the man that comes
from woman,
The womb, the teats, nipples, breast-milk, tears, laughter, weeping,
love-looks, love-perturbations and risings,
The voice, articulation, language, whispering, shouting aloud,
Food, drink, pulse, digestion, sweat, sleep, walking, swimming,
Poise on the hips, leaping, reclining, embracing, arm-curving and
tightening,
The continual changes of the flex of the mouth, and around the
eyes,
The skin, the sunburnt shade, freckles, hair,
The curious sympathy one feels when feeling with the hand the
naked meat of the body,
The circling rivers the breath, and breathing it in and out,
The beauty of the waist, and thence of the hips, and thence
downward toward the knees,
The thin red jellies within you or within me, the bones and the
marrow in the bones,
The exquisite realization of health;
O I say these are not the parts and poems of the body only, but of
the soul,
O I say now these are the soul!

Figs

D. H. Lawrence

The proper way to eat a fig, in society,
Is to split it in four, holding it by the stump,
And open it, so that it is a glittering, rosy, moist, honied, heavy-
  petalled four-petalled flower.

Then you throw away the skin
Which is just like a four-sepalled calyx,
After you have taken off the blossom, with your lips.

But the vulgar way
Is just to put your mouth to the crack, and take out the flesh in
  one bite.

Every fruit has its secret.

The fig is a very secretive fruit.
As you see it standing growing, you feel at once it is symbolic:
And it seems male.
But when you come to know it better, you agree with the Romans,
  it is female.

The Italians vulgarly say, it stands for the female part; the fig-fruit:
The fissure, the yoni,
The wonderful moist conductivity towards the centre.

Involved,
Inturned,
The flowering all inward and womb-fibrilled;
And but one orifice.

The fig, the horse-shoe, the squash-blossom.
Symbols.

There was a flower that flowered inward, womb-ward;
Now there is a fruit like a ripe womb.

It was always a secret.
That's how it should be, the female should always be secret.

There never was any standing aloft and unfolded on a bough
Like other flowers, in a revelation of petals;
Silver-pink peach, venetian green glass of medlars and sorb-apples,
Shallow wine-cups on short, bulging stems
Openly pledging heaven:
Here's to the thorn in flower! Here is to Utterance!
The brave, adventurous rosaceæ.

Folded upon itself, and secret unutterable,
And milky-sapped, sap that curdles milk and makes *ricotta*,
Sap that smells strange on your fingers, that even goats won't taste it;
Folded upon itself, enclosed like any Mohammedan woman,
Its nakedness all within-walls, its flowering forever unseen,
One small way of access only, and this close-curtained from the
    light;
Fig, fruit of the female mystery, covert and inward,
Mediterranean fruit, with your covert nakedness,
Where everything happens invisible, flowering and fertilization,
    and fruiting
In the inwardness of your you, that eye will never see
Till it's finished, and you're over-ripe, and you burst to give up
    your ghost.

Till the drop of ripeness exudes,
And the year is over.

And then the fig has kept her secret long enough.
So it explodes, and you see through the fissure the scarlet.
And the fig is finished, the year is over.

That's how the fig dies, showing her crimson through the
    purple slit
Like a wound, the exposure of her secret, on the open day.
Like a prostitute, the bursten fig, making a show of her secret.

That's how women die too.

The year is fallen over-ripe,
The year of our women.
The year of our women is fallen over-ripe.
The secret is laid bare.
And rottenness soon sets in.
The year of our women is fallen over-ripe.

When Eve once knew *in her mind* that she was naked
She quickly sewed fig-leaves, and sewed the same for the man.
She'd been naked all her days before,
But till then, till that apple of knowledge, she hadn't had the fact
    on her mind.

She got the fact on her mind, and quickly sewed fig-leaves.
And women have been sewing ever since.
But now they stitch to adorn the bursten fig, not to cover it.
They have their nakedness more than ever on their mind,
And they won't let us forget it.

Now, the secret
Becomes an affirmation through moist, scarlet lips
That laugh at the Lord's indignation.

What then, good Lord! cry the women.
We have kept our secret long enough.
We are a ripe fig.
Let us burst into affirmation.

They forget, ripe figs won't keep.
Ripe figs won't keep.

Honey-white figs of the north, black figs with scarlet inside, of the
    south.
Ripe figs won't keep, won't keep in any clime.
What then, when women the world over have all bursten into
    affirmation?
And bursten figs won't keep?

Animal, Vegetable, Mineral

Naomi Foyle

With wincing scissors
he trims my chestnut bush,
saving tufts of old growth
for burning on the heath.

When I'm bristling
like a coconut,
he lathers up the shaving brush
on a coin of Fenland soap –

surrounding my mound
with foam,
and scraping his razor
into the scree,

he draws a vulpine muzzle
down upon my lips.
My clit sticks out pink
like a tongue tip

as with my gummy muscles
I grip his index finger:
hungry as a fox cub
nursed by a human mother.

Eve to the Serpent

Catherine Smith

Stretched on tiptoes, knowing
your eyes are flickering over me –
at my sex especially – look
how I twist the stalk
and snap – pluck it carefully,
because it is precious,
unblemished, and wrong.
I've never been more curious
than this. I think about the skin,
how my teeth will rip into it,
about the flesh, how clean
and white it will be, how luscious.
You told me, didn't you? –
it will be the most delicious thing
I've ever put in my mouth,
its juice a drizzle of nectar.
It will do me so much good.
I might just stand here with it
in my hand, while you writhe
and sweat in your ornamental skin,
your tongue quivering. This could be
the longest afternoon of our lives.

A Woman Waits for Me

Walt Whitman

A woman waits for me, she contains all, nothing is lacking,
Yet all were lacking if sex were lacking, or if the moisture of
   the right man were lacking.

Sex contains all, bodies, souls,
Meanings, proofs, purities, delicacies, results, promulgations,
Songs, commands, health, pride, the maternal mystery, the
   seminal milk,
All hopes, benefactions, bestowals, all the passions, loves,
   beauties, delights of the earth,
All the governments, judges, gods, follow'd persons of the
   earth,
These are contain'd in sex as parts of itself and justifications
   of itself.

Without shame the man I like knows and avows the
   deliciousness of his sex,
Without shame the woman I like knows and avows hers.

Now I will dismiss myself from impassive women,
I will go stay with her who waits for me, and with those
   women that are warm-blooded sufficient for me,
I see that they understand me and do not deny me,
I see that they are worthy of me, I will be the robust
   husband of those women.

They are not one jot less than I am,
They are tann'd in the face by shining suns and blowing
   winds,

Their flesh has the old divine suppleness and strength,
They know how to swim, row, ride, wrestle, shoot, run,
    strike, retreat, advance, resist, defend themselves,
They are ultimate in their own right – they are calm, clear,
    well-possess'd of themselves.

I draw you close to me, you women,
I cannot let you go, I would do you good,
I am for you, and you are for me, not only for our own
    sake, but for others' sakes,
Envelop'd in you sleep greater heroes and bards,
They refuse to awake at the touch of any man but me.

It is I, you women, I make my way,
I am stern, acrid, large, undissuadable, but I love you,
I do not hurt you any more than is necessary for you,
I pour the stuff to start sons and daughters fit for these
    States, I press with slow rude muscle,
I brace myself effectually, I listen to no entreaties,
I dare not withdraw till I deposit what has so long
    accumulated within me.

Through you I drain the pent-up rivers of myself,
In you I wrap a thousand onward years,
On you I graft the grafts of the best-beloved of me and
    America,
The drops I distil upon you shall grow fierce and athletic
    girls, new artists, musicians, and singers,
The babes I beget upon you are to beget babes in their turn,
I shall demand perfect men and women out of my love-
    spendings,

I shall expect them to interpenetrate with others,
    as I and you interpenetrate now,
I shall count on the fruits of the gushing showers of them, as
    I count on the fruits of the gushing showers I give now,
I shall look for loving crops from the birth, life, death,
    immortality, I plant so lovingly now.

My Black Triangle

Grace Nichols

My black triangle
sandwiched between the geography of my thighs

Is a Bermuda
of tiny atoms
forever seizing
and releasing
the world

My black triangle
is so rich
that it flows over
on to the dry crotch
of the world

My black triangle
is black light
sitting on the threshold
of the world

Overlooking deep-pink
probabilities

and though
it spares a thought
for history
my black triangle
has spread beyond his story
beyond the dry fears of parch-ri-archy

spreading and growing
trusting and flowering
my black triangle
carries the seal of approval
of my deepest self

2

'Also those desires glowing openly'

'If you were coming in the fall'

Emily Dickinson

If you were coming in the fall,
I'd brush the summer by
With half a smile and half a spurn,
As housewives do a fly.

If I could see you in a year,
I'd wind the months in balls,
And put them each in separate drawers,
Until their time befalls.

If only centuries delayed,
I'd count them on my hand,
Subtracting till my fingers dropped
Into Van Diemen's land.

If certain, when this life was out,
That yours and mine should be,
I'd toss it yonder like a rind,
And taste eternity.

But now, all ignorant of the length
Of time's uncertain wing,
It goads me, like the goblin bee,
That will not state its sting.

'First, I want to make you come in my hand'

Marilyn Hacker

First, I want to make you come in my hand
while I watch you and kiss you, and if you cry,
I'll drink your tears while, with my whole hand, I
hold your drenched loveliness contracting. And
after a breath, I want to make you full
again, and wet. I want to make you come
in my mouth like a storm. No tears now. The sum
of your parts is my whole most beautiful
chart of the constellations – your left breast
in my mouth again. You know you'll have to be
your age. As I lie beside you, cover me
like a gold cloud, hands everywhere, at last
inside me where I trust you, then your tongue
where I need you. I want you to make me come.

Non Sum Qualis Eram Bonae Sub Regno Cynarae

Ernest Dowson

Last night, ah, yesternight, betwixt her lips and mine
There fell thy shadow, Cynara! thy breath was shed
Upon my soul between the kisses and the wine;
And I was desolate and sick of an old passion,
Yea, I was desolate and bowed my head:
I have been faithful to thee, Cynara! in my fashion.

All night upon mine heart I felt her warm heart beat,
Night-long within mine arms in love and sleep she lay;
Surely the kisses of her bought red mouth were sweet;
But I was desolate and sick of an old passion,
When I awoke and found the dawn was gray:
I have been faithful to thee, Cynara! in my fashion.

I have forgot much, Cynara! gone with the wind,
Flung roses, roses riotously with the throng,
Dancing, to put thy pale, lost lilies out of mind;
But I was desolate and sick of an old passion,
Yea, all the time, because the dance was long:
I have been faithful to thee, Cynara! in my fashion.

I cried for madder music and for stronger wine,
But when the feast is finished and the lamps expire,
Then falls thy shadow, Cynara! the night is thine;
And I am desolate and sick of an old passion,
Yea, hungry for the lips of my desire:
I have been faithful to thee, Cynara! in my fashion.

I Feel

Elizabeth Jennings

I feel I could be turned to ice
If this goes on, if this goes on.
I feel I could be buried twice
And still the death not yet be done.

I feel I could be turned to fire
If there can be no end to this.
I know within me such desire
No kiss could satisfy, no kiss.

I feel I could be turned to stone,
A solid block not carved at all,
Because I feel so much alone.
I could be grave-stone or a wall.

But better to be turned to earth
Where other things at least can grow.
I could be then a part of birth,
Passive, not knowing how to know.

He Asked About the Quality

C. P. Cavafy

From the office where he'd been taken on
to fill a position that was trivial and poorly paid
(eight pounds a month, including bonus) –
he emerged as soon as he'd finished the dreary tasks
that kept him bent over his desk all afternoon.
At seven he came out and began to stroll
slowly down the street. He was handsome
in an interesting way, with the look of a man
who had reached the peak of his sensual potential.
He'd turned twenty-nine a month before.

He dawdled along the street, then down
the shabby alleys that led to his apartment.

As he passed a little shop that sold cheap
imitation goods for workmen,
inside he saw a face, a physique
that urged him on, and in he walked,
inquiring about some coloured handkerchiefs.

He asked about the quality of the handkerchiefs
and what they cost; his voice
breaking, almost stifled by desire.
The answers came back in the same tone,
distracted, the low timbre
suggesting veiled consent.

They went on talking about the merchandise –
but their sole aim was for their hands to touch
over the handkerchiefs, for their faces,
their lips, as if by chance, to brush against each other:
for some momentary contact of the flesh.

Swiftly and in secret, so that the shop owner,
seated at the back, would never notice.

Trans. Avi Sharon

Guacamole

Kaddy Benyon

Avocados were somewhere on the lust-list
we made sated on the floor of room 404.
Write down, you said, *write down every wicked
little dirty thing you'd like us to try.* I pitted
the felt-tip against my teeth, then whispered:
*I want you to carefully split a ripe avocado,
loosen its pip, scoop out the warm yellowy
flesh and squeeze it to a gentle pulp, then –*

I stopped – back suddenly at my mother's side,
eye-level with hip and kitchen top, glued to
her hands as she cuts and twists the wizened pears,
mashes in garlic, the devil-tailed chillies, a
splash of lime. Ravenous, open-mouthed, I crave
to lick the buttery mush between her fingers,
the jaded smear from her wrist, to suck her
wedding ring, to suck her wedding ring clean.

Daniel Craig: The Screensaver

Rich Goodson

. . . & when I fail to focus, when I tire,
he rises like a Christ newly baptised
in sky-blue trunks, reminding me desire
will always lie in wait & be disguised
as men with healing hands & cute-cruel lips
& arms I'd die for should they ever press
too hard against my throat.
                                                    When water drips
from him the fish swim to his feet, confess
how happily waylaid they are, congeal
in spasmic foil &, even then, mouth how
the breeding pools upstream are no big deal.

Before my eyes bake white like theirs I vow
I'll hit a key. Before I go berserk
I'll kill him with one finger. Wake up. Work.

Hypothetical

Maria Taylor

A friend of mine asked me if I'd sleep with Daniel Craig,
would I make love to him or kick him out of bed?
Before I have time to answer, I'm in bed with Daniel Craig.
He's stirring out of sleep, smelling of Tobacco Vanille,
he flatters my performance, asks if I'd like coffee.
'Hang on,' I say, 'I did not sleep with you, Daniel Craig,
this is just a conversational frolic.' My friend stands
in the corner of my bedroom, 'You've gone too far,' she says.
I'm pulling the duvet away from his Hollywood body
at exactly the moment my husband enters the room.
I say, 'Yes, this is exactly what it looks like, darling,
but it's hypothetical, a mere conversational frolic.'
He's threatening me. There are lawyers in the room.
My children begin to cry. I don't even like Daniel Craig.

It's too late. The sheets are full of secreted evidence.
There are forensics in the room, covering my body
in blue powder, checking my skin for finger prints:
they match Daniel Craig's. He doesn't even know
he's slept with me. My marriage is a dead gull.
My neighbours come into the room shaking heads
oh dear oh dear oh dear. My husband has drawn lists
of all the things he wants to keep: a plasma screen,
an Xbox, a collection of muesli-coloured pebbles
from our holidays in Truro, 'When you loved me!'
he snaps. My children will see a therapist after school.
Daniel Craig is naked in a hypothetical sense,

telling me we can make this work. My friend smirks
behind a celebrity magazine featuring lurid details
of our affair. There are photos. We are on a beach
in the Dominican Republic, healthy and tanned
both kicking sand at a playful Joan Collins.

'I don't even like Daniel Craig,' I tell the ceiling.

Found Wanting

Rosie Sandler

When you find me wanting
is it because I cry
at children's films –
how Bambi's mother
always dies and E. T.
always goes home?

Or because I never know
which way is North
or why it matters –
losing myself
in the thrill of uncertainty?

Is it my wanton honesty,
my wilful ignorance
or how I scoff
at boundaries –
regarding hedgerows
and faux-pas
with equal equanimity?

Or maybe you don't like
my singing, the way
my lungs squeeze
each note flat.

But know this:
I dream in perfect pitch –
your hands on my breasts
your lips on my thighs
my breath on your skin
my blood beating time with yours.

So, when you find me wanting,
do you suspect
that I'm wanting you
too much?

Young Men Dancing

Linda Chase

Who were those young men dancing?
And why were they dancing with you?
And what was the meaning of all that business
around the area of the pelvis, both pelvises,
I mean, since I saw you with two of them –
two men, that is, with one pelvis each.
Though there is your pelvis too, to reckon with.
It made quite a show of itself out there
on the dance floor. Not to be overlooked
nor slighted in any way, sticking like a magnet
to the erratic rhythms of those young men,
their jeans curving and cupping and making
promises in all directions of things to come.

Which way to go, you must have asked yourself
a dozen times at least, as the young man
with the smile turned this way, and the
young man with the dreamy eyes turned that,
and you were dazed, in circles, spinning
this way and that way, brushing up against them
in confusion, body parts in gentle friction
sliding back and forth, nearly seeming like
you hadn't meant to do it.
Did you mean to do it?

Could they feel your nipples harden?
Did they know what must have happened
as your thighs began to stick together, throbbing
to the music? Thank God there was the music
you could hide behind and make it look like dancing.
I'm wondering just how much attention
young men pay.

Sandcastles

Richard Scott

A tall gent waits
inside the playground
not looking at any one child

but rather mostly
at the dog-dark door
of the public lavs

and the shadows
pooling within.

I wish I could enjoy
forging sandcastles with you
and your two-year-old,

filling the lime-green bucket,
packing it down
with the luminous shovel . . .

only now this man is
watching me –

he's caught me
amongst the families,
caught me trying to play daddy.

His gaze is iron-heavy
as he walks
to the lavatory door,

pauses, like he were crossing a road,
then enters . . .

In one version of the poem I
follow him in, slide up next to the cistern.
He bolts the grimy cubicle door
behind us. Unzips my jeans.

In another I stay building with your daughter,
perfecting the castle's keep, the last place to be breached
in a siege. In another I'm disgusted by these queers
who hang around toilets trying to catch my eye.

In another I am your husband – I yearn to leave
our daughter alone for just a handful of minutes –
she'd be fine out here – knowing there is more love
for me in there, with him.

In the last version I am your daughter,
sculpting the intricate castle from damp sand
pitted through with fag ends and gum –
oblivious to the men, the poem being written.

Remember, Body . . .

C. P. Cavafy

Body, remember not only how deeply you were loved,
not only the many beds where you lay,
but also those desires that flashed
openly in their eyes
or trembled in the voice – and were thwarted
by some chance impediment.
Now that all of them are locked away in the past,
it almost seems as if you surrendered
to even those pre-empted desires – how they flashed, remember,
in the eyes of those who looked at you, how they trembled
in the voice for you, remember, body.

Trans. Avi Sharon

Love & Sex & Boys in Showers

John Whitworth

Wishing, wondering, thinking, talking,
Is it Medicine? Is it Smarties?
Difficult, like tightrope walking?
Easy, like a broken heart is?
Where the sea along the shore moans,
Hear the humming of the hormones,
Messages of meeting, parting,
Is it worth the grief of starting?
Can the sweets outweigh the sours?
Love & Sex & Boys in Showers.

Suppose I let him go too far, but
Just how far is that precisely?
Suppose we do it in the car, but
After will he treat me nicely?
Everything I want's illicit,
Adult, sexually explicit.
When he stuns me with his kisses,
Sweet as Sugar, bold as Bliss is,
Will I savour them for hours?
Love & Sex & Boys in Showers.

Steamy dreams of saltlick shoulders,
Peach-fuzz thighs and silky bottom.
Hearts have reasons. They're as old as
Time. I swear I think I've got 'em.
Shy and shyer, fond and fonder,
There, where ocean meets blue yonder,
Skinnydips on desert island,
Wisechild wideness of his smile and
Lotus blossoms, passion flowers,
Love & Sex & Boys in Showers.

Princesses are racked and gloomy,
Fated, dated, triste and tragic.
Lose a few and draw a few – my
Life's like football. Football's magic.
Choose the time, the place, the weapons.
Karma's just the shit that happens,
Everything we have is ours,
We've got paranormal powers,
Princesses are shut in towers,
Love & Sex & Boys in Showers.

Service

Gregory Woods

For all that he's a sullen brute,
His pout is cute. In silhouette
The bursting of a rotten fruit,
It putters, muttering his fret,
Expressive though completely mute.
His lips could flay a clarinet,
His tongue electrocute a flute.
Worth challenging to a duet,
With fists like his he could transmute
A fight into a minuet,
A blunderbuss into a lute.
Within some squalid oubliette
He strips down to his birthday suit –
Tattoo and hand-rolled cigarette.
The remnants of his ill-repute –
His nakedness no less a threat
Than uniformed in hot pursuit
Of somebody to shoot or pet,
More rigid than in full salute.
How could one get this dun cadet
To proffer if not prostitute
Himself; develop the coquette
Within the manly absolute?
I'd tempt him to forget regret,
That fetter to the dissolute;
To whet his appetite, I'd let

Him flatten me with his hirsute
Anatomy, the better yet
His persecution to refute;
I'd lick his feet (sweet etiquette!),
Recruit his sweat, and substitute
His carcan with a carcanet.

O Little One

Marilyn Hacker

O little one, this longing is the pits.
I'm horny as a timber wolf in heat.
Three times a night, I tangle up the sheet.
I seem to flirt with everything with tits:
Karyn at lunch, who knows I think she's cute;
my ex, the DA on the Sex Crimes Squad;
Iva's gnarled, canny New England god-
mother, who was my Saturday night date.
I'm trying to take things one at a time:
Situps at bedtime, less coffee, less meat,
more showers, till a remedy appears.
Since there's already quite enough Sex Crime,
I think I ought to be kept off the street.
What are you doing for the next five years?

Troilism

Roddy Lumsden

I could mention X, locked naked
in the spare room by two so taken
with each other, they no longer needed him,

or Y who, with an erection in either hand,
said she felt like she was skiing,
or Z who woke in a hotel bed in a maze

of shattered champagne glass
between two hazy girls, his wallet light.
Me? I never tried it, though like many

I thought and thought about it
until a small moon rose above a harvest field,
which was satisfying, in its own way, enough.

Assurance

Emma Lazarus

Last night I slept, and when I woke her kiss
Still floated on my lips. For we had strayed
Together in my dream, through some dim glade,
Where the shy moonbeams scarce dared light our bliss.
The air was dank with dew, between the trees,
The hidden glow-worms kindled and were spent.
Cheek pressed to cheek, the cool, the hot night-breeze
Mingled our hair, our breath, and came and went,
As sporting with our passion. Low and deep
Spake in mine ear her voice: 'And didst thou dream,
This could be buried? This could be sleep?
And love be thrall to death! Nay, whatso seem,
Have faith, dear heart; *this is the thing that is*!'
Thereon I woke, and on my lips her kiss.

Losing It to David Cassidy

Catherine Smith

That hot evening, all through our clumsy fuck,
David smiled down from the wall. His ironed hair,
American teeth. Eyes on me, his best girl.

And his fingers didn't smell of smoke, he didn't
nudge me onto my back, like you did, grunting
as he unzipped my jeans, complaining

you're so bony, and demanding, *Now you do something –
hold it like this*. David took my virginity
in a room scented with white roses, having smoothed

the sheets himself, slotted 'How Can I be Sure?'
into the tape machine. And when we were done
he didn't roll off, zip up and slouch downstairs

to watch the end of *Match of the Day* with my brother,
oh no, not David. He washed me, patted me dry
with fat blue towels, his eyes brim-full of tears.

A Man Greets His Wife from Her Short Break Away

Rebecca Goss

The first thing they do is embrace.
Fat smiles stay on their faces
all the way to the restaurant.

He eats ribs with sticky, podgy fingers.
She bites chicken wings with shiny lips.
They have a pudding each and share another.

In the car, she tells him about a girl she saw,
with a short, spotted skirt that flapped
around one long limb.

'There wasn't even a stump to satisfy me,
just a space where the leg should've been.'
'Was she very pretty?'

'Yes she was.'
They stop talking and at traffic lights
he strokes her thigh, instead of saying

how sad her story sounds. Quietly, he resents the one-legged girl
for changing the mood between them, resents his wife
for telling him the tale at all.

Making love to her later, it's a pretty teenager
sitting astride his wide belly. One leg tucked behind,
leaving the torso, smooth and deformed, moving over him.

Wanting to Think

Michael Schmidt

Why, when I want to think of you, do I think of him?
He may be dead, and yet he still lies with you
Warming his calloused hands between your thighs.
He may still be alive, and his lips for ever
Puckered on your nipple, above your heart.

I want to think about you in my arms, the way we were
For a while. Then he came out of nowhere to stay.
He was tall, and golden, stripped to the waist, when we sawed
And chopped all autumn the firewood, heaped it
Outside your kitchen door. You were always watching;

You patted him on the back and sniffed the air
Pungent with our sweat, you caught his smell.
That autumn, when I lay with you, you started pretending
These hands of mine were his hands in the dark, these lips
His and the tufts in my armpits his and you inhaled

Hungry, pressed against me, pressed against
A man you were imagining in my place:
Shaping, stretching me to fit your bed; no wonder
When I think of you, as I do, each day and night, I think
Of what you were thinking of, how you watched as I watched you,

How as autumn ended, just before you left
That night, noiseless, away with him for good,
I came upon him at twilight in a clearing.
After the weeks we'd mutely worked together,
Till dark we rested in the deep cool grass without a word.

While all the time I loved you, as I love you,
He lay with me and he was satisfied,
I lay with him and not for a minute thought
Of how you watched through the screen door, but only
How musky, how good he smelled, and his hand on my chest.

3

'A night picked from a hundred and one'

Imperial

Don Paterson

Is it normal to get this wet? Baby, I'm frightened –
I covered her mouth with my own;
she lay in my arms till the storm-window brightened
and stood at our heads like a stone

After months of jaw-jaw, determined that neither
win ground, or be handed the edge,
we gave ourselves up, one to the other
like prisoners over a bridge

and no trade was ever so fair or so tender;
so where was the flaw in the plan,
the night we lay down on the flag of surrender
and woke on the flag of Japan

Viginty Alley

Tim Liardet

I was thrown, you might say, on the mercy
Of her knowledge. Were there less, there'd be plenty:
Undo this, she softly cajoled, no, this.
Miles away, her slant green eyes slid up
To the contingencies of cloud ebbing over the sidings.
When she wrote it there on the subway wall
In an unbookish hand as deep red as Chianti
She dropped, like she dropped her gaze, the r and i –
X marks the spot. Here's where the mammer's boy
Lost his viginty.

It, whatever it was, indeed was lost
Along with the gormless and the donkey-voiced,
Along with all sense of ingenuous folly
Once the chemicals started to boil in the pit.
It was lost there, or left, or merely discarded
Like creaky, unbroken shoes, like out-of-season holly.
It was lost, or merely dumped
Along with everything else no longer of use
Down at the deep end of Viginty Alley.

Outside

Robert Frant

I thought you'd stop my searching touch
Although you wanted just as much
To have me on this crowded route;
Your denim skirt, my soft dark suit,

But even though we could be seen
I ached to feel myself between
Your legs, to sense the moistness there
For me if I would only dare.

I slid your skirt above your hips,
Your naked neck against my lips
Then eased my hardness into you.
A gasp, a moan, my hardness grew.

The people never dropped their pace
Not knowing that our close embrace
Was hiding something known to just
We two: our deep, impatient lust.

Amores 1.5

Ovid

A hot afternoon: siesta-time. Exhausted,
  I lay sprawled across my bed.
One window-shutter was closed, the other stood half-open,
  And the light came sifting through
As it does in a wood. It recalled that crepuscular glow at sunset
  Or the trembling moment between darkness and dawn,
Just right for a modest girl whose delicate bashfulness
  Needs some camouflage. And then –
In stole Corinna, long hair tumbled about her
  Soft white throat, a rustle of summer skirts,
Like some fabulous Eastern queen *en route* to her
    bridal-chamber –
  Or a top-line city call-girl, out on the job.
I tore the dress off her – not that it really hid much,
  But all the same she struggled to keep it on:
Yet her efforts were unconvincing, she seemed half-hearted –
  Inner self-betrayal made her give up.
When at last she stood naked before me, not a stitch of clothing,
  I couldn't fault her body at any point.
Smooth shoulders, delectable arms (I saw, I touched them),
  Nipples inviting caresses, the flat
Belly outlined beneath that flawless bosom,
  Exquisite curve of a hip, firm youthful thighs.
But why catalogue details? Nothing came short of perfection,
  And I clasped her naked body close to mine.
Fill in the rest for yourselves! Tired at last, we lay sleeping.
  May my siestas often turn out that way!

Trans. Peter Green

The Wasp Station

Paul Johnston

He was sixteen, she in her forties – the classic older woman
scenario, though her hair was shorter than Anne Bancroft's
and he wasn't such a dork as Dustin Hoffman.

They didn't do it in a hotel but in a garden shed, rusty
sickles, shovels and old model railway bits all around.
A wasp was hitting the buffers on the web-wrought window.

His lack of experience hung off him like a fireman's uniform
as he stammered, bruised lips when he kissed her and grabbed
for her breasts when she ground their groins together.

She opened her blouse and let him lap the c-cup cornucopia,
her nipples rigid as funnels. It was obvious that squeezing his rod
would bring him juddering to the terminus faster than the Flying
    Scot.

'Now we take our time,' she said, reginal. 'Yes, ma'am,' his look
bolder despite the stickiness in his boxers. He stripped them off
and wiped himself, then tapped his rapidly rising tool
against her whiter-than-the-driven-steam knickers.

She pulled aside the gusset and let him in. All aboard!
They rode the Orient Express to Paris, Venice, Istanbul,
cities on fire with carnal pleasure. She shrieked as they entered
the tunnel, pistons thundering and steam cocks fully open.

She arrived first, bucking, nails digging into his coal tender.
He squealed and spurted, head back like a plume of wind-whipped
    smoke,
then panted in her ear, 'I love you, Aunt Alice.' She looked away;

the wasp was tangled in the silken threads, its movements
    lacking vim,
its screech the desperate braking of a soon-to-be-derailed express.
'Silly boy,' she said, reversing. 'I'll see you here tomorrow, same
    time.'
Having deposited, she thought, my underwear in a left luggage
    locker.

He grinned, wondering where his uncle and cousins were; and
    would be
the next day. Roger at his office near St Pancras, Lily
and Jez blowing out clouds of skunk in the park?

The wasp manages to jab the spider's belly with its stinger
and in a single tug is free, a sentient yellow-and-black
bullet racketing past them to the station exit.

And Looking Back

A. F. Harrold

Sometimes a hand in or of or from the past can make us come
alive again without our realising what it is that's being done.

And sometimes bodies find their ways from where they each
    began,
a surprise curving into the present, into the light, under the hand,
and without warning or comment everything on hold has suddenly
    begun
and now, it seems, this is not as bad as it could possibly have
    become
and for a while there's only time and flesh to pass before the
    rising sun.

And it happens that tonight is a night picked from a hundred
    and one
other possible nights, each spinning lost between the stars in the
    silence from
the closing mouths of kisses and answers and the lover's tongue
to the morning that in the end is well known to always come.

And looking back what is there that has not yet been remarked
    upon,
the resistance of memory to education of any form,
or the ritual days of living that nights like this can pluck us from?

Explode

John Etchingham

It's the way that you say 'I don't usually do this'
And seeing your pain all the time mixed with such bliss,
Initial resistance both mental and physical,
Tightness that gives way to depths almost mystical;

Slowly at first, just until you get used to me –
Pushing, I feel you relax so deliciously,
Urging me on I try not to let go, but who
Could keep control? I just have to explode in you.

The Man in the Print Room

Sarah Salway

Now if he's slow and she gets upset
he'll move towards her, tease the hair
from her face, lick her tears away.

She lets him tie the straps on her new ankle boots,
teaches him to pull her corset just tight enough,
has sewn fifty pearl buttons on a black sheath dress
he presses into her skin like the photocopier code.

All day she hugs the thought of him close,
how he knows the word of more in every tongue.

La Noche Oscura

San Juan de la Cruz

En una noche oscura,
con ansias en amores inflamada,
(¡oh dichosa ventura!)
salí sin ser notada,
estando ya mi casa sosegada.

A oscuras y segura,
por la secreta escala disfrazada,
(¡oh dichosa ventura!)
a oscuras y en celada,
estando ya mi casa sosegada.

En la noche dichosa,
en secreto, que nadie me veía,
ni yo miraba cosa,
sin otra luz ni guía
sino la que en el corazón ardía.

Aquésta me guïaba
más cierta que la luz del mediodía,
adonde me esperaba
quien yo bien me sabía,
en parte donde nadie parecía.

¡Oh noche que me guiaste!,
¡oh noche amable más que el alborada!,
¡oh noche que juntaste
amado con amada,
amada en el amado transformada!

En mi pecho florido,
que entero para él solo se guardaba,
allí quedó dormido,
y yo le regalaba,
y el ventalle de cedros aire daba.

El aire de la almena,
cuando yo sus cabellos esparcía,
con su mano serena
en mi cuello hería,
y todos mis sentidos suspendía.

Quedéme y olvidéme,
el rostro recliné sobre el amado,
cesó todo, y dejéme,
dejando mi cuidado
entre las azucenas olvidado.

Dark Night

On a dark night,
Kindled in love with yearnings
– oh, happy chance! –
I went forth without being observed,
My house being now at rest.

In darkness and secure,
By the secret ladder, disguised
– oh, happy chance! –
In darkness and in concealment,
My house being now at rest.

In the happy night,
In secret, when none saw me,
Nor I beheld aught,
Without light or guide,
save that which burned in my heart.

This light guided me
More surely than the light of noonday
To the place where he
(well I knew who!) was awaiting me –
A place where none appeared.

Oh, night that guided me,
Oh, night more lovely than the dawn,
Oh, night that joined
Beloved with lover,
Lover transformed in the Beloved!

Upon my flowery breast,
Kept wholly for himself alone,
There he stayed sleeping,
and I caressed him,
And the fanning of the cedars made a breeze.

The breeze blew from the turret
As I parted his locks;
With his gentle hand
He wounded my neck
And caused all my senses to be suspended.

I remained, lost in oblivion;
My face I reclined on the Beloved.
All ceased and I abandoned myself,
Leaving my cares
forgotten among the lilies.

i like my body

e. e. cummings

i like my body when it is with your
body. It is so quite new a thing.
Muscles better and nerves more.
i like your body. i like what it does,
i like its hows. i like to feel the spine
of your body and its bones, and the trembling
-firm-smooth ness and which i will
again and again and again
kiss, i like kissing this and that of you,
i like, slowly stroking the, shocking fuzz
of your electric fur, and what-is-it comes
over parting flesh . . . And eyes big love-crumbs,

and possibly i like the thrill

of under me you so quite new

Ur Thurs Reidh Ansur

Ros Barber

To you, I taste like sin; tobacco and alcohol
mingling hot-foul and exotic. I get you drunk
against your better judgement, and as I lead you
out, you sway, say no, giddy with the inevitable.

You like beaches? I've made love by the Med,
the Channel, the North Atlantic. Then you
follow me onto the abandoned shingle,
the daylight biting your retina. It is too cold

to undress, and when I swallow your cock
(my mouth so hot it makes you dizzy) you
thrust your numb fingers into my coat
to find my breasts. So you're a poet,

I whisper, sensing your balls tighten
under my gloves. Please, you reply.
Mute, I push your head down,
you are thirsty, I know you can taste

this morning's bath, but traces too
of another man's semen, blood,
the dampness of seaweed.
The tide is pushing itself towards us;

a man walking his dog unzips
his anorak. I straddle you, we sit
rocking in the breeze, dialect thick on your
lips, saliva stringing between us. Please,

please. I smile and your eyes roll back
with the receding grasp of breakers.
You're no longer making any sense
to me; something like Old Norse

retches in your throat as the hot rush
releases you. Afterwards you mutter faintly,
half-metre, near rhyme, kissing my neck as your
poems seep away into the shingle.

Punctuation

Claire Dyer

We're making love and there's a comma on your shoulder.
It's shining in the dark –

part pause, part the start of separation.
Question marks are in your eyes.

I have no answer other than to press my lips
to your neck and feel you smile.

This moment's stolen, we're living in quotation marks.
Next you touch me with apostrophes –

silky on my skin, they brush my breasts with belonging.
I arch my back, our release is an exclamation.

Afterwards, the sheet's littered with semicolons,
colons, there are hyphens between our toes

and we speak ellipsis, promise each other
a lexicon without a word for grief, or any full stop –

On being in Bed with Your Brand-new Lover

Amy Key

I've abandoned vanity, since I became a body
of threads, never quite made, since you rippled
the apparent skin of me.

I'm all texture. Silk rosette, billowing coral,
tentative as a just baked cake. Sensations
slide over my knitted blood.

My mouth is a glass paperweight
to keep our tastes in, like maraschino
cherries and water from a zinc cup.

The Platonic Blow (A Day for a Lay)

W. H. Auden

It was a spring day, a day, a day for a lay when the air
Smelled like a locker-room, a day to blow or get blown.
Returning from lunch I turned my corner and there
On a near-by stoop I saw him standing alone.

I glanced as I advanced. The clean white T-shirt outlined
A forceful torso, the light-blue denims divulged
Much. I observed the snug curves where they hugged the behind,
I watched the crotch where the cloth intriguingly bulged.

Our eyes met, I felt sick. My knees turned weak.
I couldn't move. I didn't know what to say.
In a blur I heard words myself like a stranger speak.
'Will you come to my room?' Then a husky voice, 'O.K.'

I produced some beer and we talked. Like a little boy
He told me his story. Present address next door.
Half Polish half Irish The youngest. From Illinois.
Profession mechanic. Name Bud. Age twenty-four.

He put down his glass and stretched his bare arms along
The back of my sofa. The afternoon sunlight struck
The blond hairs on the wrist near my head. His chin was strong,
His mouth sucky. I could hardly believe my luck.

And here he was sitting beside me, legs apart.
I could bear it no longer. I touched the inside of his thigh.
His reply was to move closer. I trembled. My heart
Thumped and jumped as my fingers went to his fly.

I opened a gap in the flap. I went in there.
I sought for a slit in the gripper shorts that had charge
Of the basket I asked for. I came to warm flesh then to hair,
I went on. I found what I hoped. I groped. It was large.

He responded to my fondling in a charming, disarming way:
Without a word he unbuckled his belt while I felt
And lolled back, stretching his legs. His pants fell away.
Carefully drawing it out, I beheld what I held.

The circumcised head was a work of mastercraft,
With perfectly beveled rim of unusual weight
And the friendliest red. Even relaxed, the shaft
Was of noble dimensions with the wrinkles that indicate

Singular powers of extension. For a second or two,
It lay there inert then suddenly stirred in my hand,
Then paused as if frightened or doubtful of what to do,
And then with a violent jerk began to expand.

By soundless bounds it extended and distended, by quick
Great leaps it rose, it flushed, it rushed to its full size.
Nearly nine inches long and three inches thick,
A royal column ineffably solemn and wise.

I tested its length and strength with a manual squeeze,
I bunched my fingers and twirled them about the knob,
I stroked it from top to bottom. I got on my knees.
I lowered my head. I opened my mouth for the job.

But he pushed me gently away. He bent down. He unlaced
His shoes. He removed his socks. Stood up. Shed
His pants altogether. Muscles in arms and waist
Rippled as he whipped his T-shirt over his head.

I scanned his tan, enjoyed the contrast of brown
Trunk against white shorts taut around small
Hips. With a dig and a wriggle he peeled them down.
I tore off my clothes. He faced me smiling. I saw all.

The gorgeous organ stood stiffly and straightly out
With a slight flare upwards. At each beat of his heart it threw
An odd little nod my way. From the slot of the spout
Exuded a drop of transparent viscous goo.

The lair of hair was fair, the grove of a young man,
A tangle of curls and whorls, luxuriant but couth.
Except for a spur of golden hairs that fan
To the neat navel, the rest of the belly was smooth.

Well hung, slung from the fork of the muscular legs,
The firm vase of his sperm, like a bulging pear,
Cradling its handsome glands, two herculean eggs,
Swung as he came towards me, shameless, bare.

We aligned mouths. We entwined. All act was clutch,
All fact contact, the attack and the interlock
Of tongues, the charms of arms. I shook at the touch
Of his fresh flesh, I rocked at the shock of his cock.

Straddling my legs a little I inserted his divine
Person between and closed on it tight as I could.
The upright warmth of his belly lay all along mine.
Nude, glued together for a minute, we stood.

I stroked the lobes of his ears, the back of his head
And the broad shoulders. I took bold hold of the compact
Globes of his bottom. We tottered. He fell on the bed.
Lips parted, eyes closed, he lay there, ripe for the act.

Mad to be had, to be felt and smelled. My lips
Explored the adorable masculine tits. My eyes
Assessed the chest. I caressed the athletic hips
And the slim limbs. I approved the grooves of the thighs.

I hugged, I snuggled into an armpit.
I sniffed the subtle whiff of its tuft. I lapped up the taste
Of its hot hollow. My fingers began to drift
On a trek of inspection, a leisurely tour of the waist.

Downward in narrowing circles they playfully strayed.
Encroached on his privates like poachers, approached the prick.
But teasingly swerved, retreated from meeting. It betrayed
Its pleading need by a pretty imploring kick.

'Shall I rim you?' I whispered. He shifted his limbs in assent,
Turned on his side and opened his legs, let me pass
To the dark parts behind. I kissed as I went
The great thick cord that ran back from his balls to his arse.

Prying the buttocks aside, I nosed my way in
Down the shaggy slopes. I came to the puckered goal.
It was quick to my licking. He pressed his crotch to my chin.
His thighs squirmed as my tongue wormed in his hole.

His sensations yearned for consummation. He untucked
His legs and lay panting, hot as a teen-age boy.
Naked, enlarged, charged, aching to get sucked,
Clawing the sheet, all his pores open to joy.

I inspected his erection. I surveyed his parts with a stare
From scrotum level. Sighting along the underside
Of his cock, I looked through the forest of pubic hair
To the range of the chest beyond rising lofty and wide.

I admired the texture, the delicate wrinkles and the neat
Sutures of the capacious bag. I adored the grace
Of the male genitalia. I raised the delicious meat
Up to my mouth, brought the face of its hard-on to my face.

Slipping my lips round the Byzantine dome of the head,
With the tip of my tongue I caressed the sensitive groove.
He thrilled to the trill. 'That's lovely!' he hoarsely said.
'Go on! Go on!' Very slowly I started to move.

Gently, intently, I slid to the massive base
Of his tower of power, paused there a moment down
In the warm moist thicket, then began to retrace
Inch by inch the smooth way to the throbbing crown.

Indwelling excitements swelled at delights to come
As I descended and ascended those thick distended walls.
I grasped his root between left forefinger and thumb
And with my right hand tickled his heavy voluminous balls.

I plunged with a rhythmical lunge steady and slow,
And at every stroke made a corkscrew roll with my tongue.
His soul reeled in the feeling. He whimpered, 'Oh!'
As I tongued and squeezed and rolled and tickled and swung.

Then I pressed on the spot where the groin is joined to the cock,
Slipped a finger into his arse and massaged him from inside.
The secret sluices of his juices began to unlock.
He melted into what he felt. 'O Jesus!' he cried.

Waves of immeasurable pleasures mounted his member in quick
Spasms. I lay still in the notch of his crotch inhaling his sweat
His ring convulsed round my finger. Into me, rich and thick,
His hot spunk spouted in gouts, spurted in jet after jet.

Rhetorical Questions

Hugo Williams

How do you think I feel
when you make me talk to you
and won't let me stop
till the words turn into a moan?
Do you think I mind
when you put your hand over my mouth
and tell me not to move
so you can 'hear' it happening?

And how do you think I like it
when you tell me what to do
and your mouth opens
and you look straight through me?
Do you think I mind
when the blank expression comes
and you set off alone
down the hall of collapsing columns?

Haikus to Fuck to

Leo Cookman

She loses her clothes
In seconds. Out stick her tits
Then she climbs on top

My cock between lips
Day and Night, joyful sucking,
'Please cum in my mouth'

Hot, sweaty and hard
My dick in her hand, she wanks
Me to perfection

I spread her legs wide
And my head put between them
To lick her pussy

'Your cock's amazing'
'I want your dick inside me'
My cock in her cunt

'Now, cum on my tits'
'You're just so hot when you cum'
'I'm stroking myself'

It's lovely to lick
Around the dark nipples on
Her round and soft breasts

She sticks her legs out
As I fuck her so hard, she
Asks it deeper still

Ecstasy in moans
As I hammer forth, inside,
Out driving our cum

My cock soaking wet
Gloved by her slit, now dripping,
We fuck. In and out.

We shout then as I
Ejaculate inside her.
Warm, creamy and white.

I slide my spent dick
Out of her sodden, wet minge.
My lover I kiss.

Caked in each other's
Kisses and sweat, on her I
Lie. Absolute bliss.

The Sun Rising

John Donne

Busy old fool, unruly Sun,
    Why dost thou thus,
Through windows, and through curtains, call on us?
Must to thy motions lovers' seasons run?
        Saucy pedantic wretch, go chide
        Late school-boys and sour prentices,
    Go tell court-huntsmen that the king will ride,
    Call country ants to harvest offices;
Love, all alike, no season knows nor clime,
Nor hours, days, months, which are the rags of time.

    Thy beams so reverend, and strong
        Why shouldst thou think?
I could eclipse and cloud them with a wink,
But that I would not lose her sight so long.
        If her eyes have not blinded thine,
        Look, and to-morrow late tell me,
    Whether both th' Indias of spice and mine
    Be where thou left'st them, or lie here with me.
Ask for those kings whom thou saw'st yesterday,
And thou shalt hear, 'All here in one bed lay.'

She's all states, and all princes I;
        Nothing else is;
Princes do but play us; compared to this,
All honour's mimic, all wealth alchemy.
        Thou, Sun, art half as happy as we,
        In that the world's contracted thus;
    Thine age asks ease, and since thy duties be
    To warm the world, that's done in warming us.
Shine here to us, and thou art everywhere;
This bed thy center is, these walls thy sphere.

Flicker

Robert Frant

Your tongue gives such pleasure
When you, at your leisure,
Form words that I treasure –
Such filth, without measure.

Then later, the flicker,
First slowly then quicker,
Addictive as liquor,
Still making me thicker

And harder inside you;
Your mouth, open wide to
Take all I provide through
Your lips as I ride you.

4

'All our states united'

Tying the Knots

Anna-May Laugher

On Audrey's wedding night
she took a pin to bed;
stabbed her finger in the breathless dark
and dabbed the linen of the 'breaking cloth'.

She made small sounds that passed for pain,
not sure it was enough, she stabbed again,
smeared a thumb-ful of redemptive blood
across the white of her stocking top.

Audrey was sixty when we met, lovely and vast,
like a dimpled sow in a yellow tabard;
always a scuff-chafe-scuff of thighs
as she mopped corridors and stairs.

Each day, once the Matins bell had stopped,
I'd wash left-greasy supper pots,
she'd squat and settle with toast and tea,
plotting lavish nuptials for her Marie.

She liked her family traditions,
the Kimber cloth for 'breaking in'.
Five generations of bridal virgins
'taken' on it by eager men.

'Well I saaaay five' she said and smiled.
'It wouldn't matter now, but then . . .'

Bicycle Pump

Irving Layton

The idle gods for laughs gave man his rump;
In sport, so made his kind that when he sighs
In ecstasy between a woman's thighs
He goes up and down, a bicycle pump;
And his beloved once his seed is sown
Swells like a faulty tube on one side blown.

Magnets

Jo Bell

Working different hours,
we settled for exchanging rude words
on the fridge.
my purple love juice spit on roses:
this member is a giant bore.

I came alone into the tired house one night
and reached for milk. I saw
I in bed now
come

Muse

Jo Bell

You show up late
in your biker jacket
hoping that a quick roll
on my laminate flooring
will remedy all ills.

It will. But make it
a good one.

The Day He Met His Wife

Peter Sansom

She said goodbye to common sense
and so they booked a room
in an afternoon hotel to holiday
with fecklessness in laundered sheets;
and there was an orchid
and a crisp new paperback,
the art gallery on a working day,
a second bottle opened and a third
knowing tomorrow in twenty years
they'd wake up with such a head,
a sink full of pots, the fridge
empty as Antarctica
and everything uphill again
in rain you could canoe
the middle of the street down,
which they did.

Conception

Sarah Salway

A winter night, his mouth on her breast
so soft the spring inside her wound tight
following the trail of it, his breath
whispering she should open up, not fight,
and she did, darling. She was one long
ache, hard to see where she ended
and he began. Then such strong
aching, hard to see where she ends
and the baby began. They become one long
whisper, opening up without a fight,
losing the trail of themselves, breath
so real the spring inside winds tight
feeling the shock of what's happening
this spring night, new mouth on her breast.

After Making Love We Hear Footsteps

Galway Kinnell

For I can snore like a bullhorn
or play loud music
or sit up talking with any reasonably sober Irishman
and Fergus will only sink deeper
into his dreamless sleep, which goes by all in one flash,
but let there be that heavy breathing
or a stifled come-cry anywhere in the house
and he will wrench himself awake
and make for it on the run – as now, we lie together,
after making love, quiet, touching along the length of our bodies,
familiar touch of the long-married,
and he appears – in his baseball pajamas, it happens,
the neck opening so small he has to screw them on –
and flops down between us and hugs us and snuggles himself to
  sleep,
his face gleaming with satisfaction at being this very child.

In the half darkness we look at each other
and smile
and touch arms across this little, startlingly muscled body –
this one whom habit of memory propels to the ground of his
  making,
sleeper only the mortal sounds can sing awake,
this blessing love gives again into our arms.

Their Sex Life

A. R. Ammons

One failure on
Top of another

Featherlite

Neil Rollinson

Waste not, want not you say as you
wring the last drops, the way
you'd get the dregs of the Burgundy
out of a wine box. You swallow the lot
like an epicure, a woman who hasn't drunk
for weeks. I see the tongue curl
in your mouth, your lips sticky and opalescent
as it runs down your throat.
An elixir, that's what you call it,
your multi-mineral and vitamin supplement:
amino acids, glucose, fructose, vitamin B12
(essential for vegetarians), vitamin C,
magnesium, calcium, potassium,
and one third of the recommended
daily dose of zinc. You wipe your chin
with a finger, and put the tip to your tongue.
The taste is acquired; like whisky,
and anchovies, you develop a passion.
It's an aphrodisiac more efficacious
than rhino horn, or Spanish Fly,
it's delicious, you say, as you grab my hair,
and push your salty tongue in my mouth.

Casanever

Nic Aubury

To most men, the notion
Of 'romance and mystery'
Means clearing the porn from
Their Internet history.

The Couple Upstairs

Nic Aubury

Their bed springs start to creak;
Their ardour has awoken.
That's twice at least this week;
Their telly must be broken.

Putting in the Seed

Robert Frost

You come to fetch me from my work to-night
When supper's on the table, and we'll see
If I can leave off burying the white
Soft petals fallen from the apple tree
(Soft petals, yes, but not so barren quite,
Mingled with these, smooth bean and wrinkled pea);
And go along with you ere you lose sight
Of what you came for and become like me,
Slave to a Springtime passion for the earth.
How Love burns through the Putting in the Seed
On through the watching for that early birth
When, just as the soil tarnishes with weed,
The sturdy seedling with arched body comes
Shouldering its way and shedding the earth crumbs.

And So Today Take Off My Wristwatch

A. F. Harrold

It has snowed and, not venturing out, it seems we must stay in,
draw the curtains back and see the winter light reflecting in
and stay in bed or share a bath and eat straight from the tin
heedless of staining the duvet which has become a sort of skin.

And with the thermostat turned up and with the wireless
    switched off
we do simply simple things that we know we do not do enough
and sometimes they have something to do with lofty things
    like love
or passion, perhaps, or loyalty, but at other times do not.

For sometimes it must be recognised that duties have stepped in
and regulated each of the hours that we have stretched between
dawn and breakfast, work and dinner and in time the heart wears
    thin.
And so today take off my wristwatch, let me lie down, breathe
    you in.

And in the silence between breathing some bird sings in the garden
and once again certain things between us start to harden.

An Epic in Me

Eva Salzman

So that the telling may not be diverse from the fact
  – Dante

Sweating, his body becomes hot wax
moulding me. I want my impression to last.

The weight of him is a team of horses
lumbering over a wooden bridge,

shoving, shoving on the advance guard.
Not quite bravery, but eloquent brawn.

He runs whole pitches through the night.
A hundred 'tries', he's no closer to goal.

Making his mark deep inside of me,
he stitches the laces of a cross, a dash –

he who loathes the intellectual.
With him I felt sublimely wordless. Until this.

Ménage à Trois

Neil Rollinson

Insatiable these mornings, full
of a drunk excitement, your eyes
have the glazed look of a woman
who hasn't slept all night; you wake me
with mouth open kisses, the smell
of a different room in your clothes.
You take off your dress and show me
the stains on your skin
like the trails of exotic gastropods;
a body paint of semen
which I rehydrate with my tongue.
I trace the splash across your stomach
and over your breast, a thick dried
river of it, flooding again; your nipple
rough with a smear of salt.
That was one hell of a shot.
I suck on you greedily and slide
my tongue where his own tongue
must have slid long into the night,
and when all trace of him is gone,
except the smell in your hair
we make our own maps on each other's skins
and we fuck like we never do
without this heat inside you, without
this ghost of a man drifting between us
like a lover sharing our bed.

Intimacy

Elizabeth Barrett

Nineteen days without you when I woke,
one morning, full with what I lacked;
laid in the bath finding evidence
of your absence and my neglect.
I shaved my underarms and legs,
plucked my eyebrows, shaped my pubes
and used my tiny scissors to snip
an errant hair. I paid attention again
to detail; tried to look at my body
the way you would – knowing
that I would drive out, that day,
to find you – that after our frantic urgency,
or that slowed motion when (somehow)
you trip it and we keep going on
and on – knowing that, after this,
you would examine every inch of me,
your blue-gray eyes drunk with it,
you rolling that one word around
your mouth like a jelly bean: *gorgeous,*
gorgeous. You're so gorgeous . . .

Later, you take my right breast
between your teeth, skim your tongue
across my nipple, ask: *Where's it gone?*
I miss it. There was just a single one.

Embrace

Rhian Gallagher

Unshowered, wrestling with the sea still on our skin
when she catches me, mid-room, with a kiss.
Not a passing glance of lips, but her intended
till I press back against the wall
laughing, in a body-search pose
as ready as her to forget about dinner.

Once, in our first months, we headed down Christopher Street
starch wafting from an open laundry, the sound of a press
squeezing a line along a sleeve. We slipped
across the West Side Highway, out on the pier
pressing our faces to the fence to catch an air of sea,
distant Liberty. Winter sun pouring its heart out
over the Hudson, she stepped into me –
the cold became a memory
smudged under our winter coats.

Two guys stood on the far side of the pier
looking baffled, how long they'd been there
god knows. Gulping, knees undone, we surfaced like swimmers
and almost ran back up Christopher Street
laughing. We'd been gone an hour, the night had come
there were shelves of lights up and down the tall streets,
she was all over me. Everything had turned on.

Topography

Sharon Olds

After we flew across the country we
got in bed, laid our bodies
delicately together, like maps laid
face to face, East to West, my
San Francisco against your New York, your
Fire Island against my Sonoma, my
New Orleans deep in your Texas, your Idaho
bright on my Great Lakes, my Kansas
burning against your Kansas your Kansas
burning against my Kansas, your Eastern
Standard Time pressing into my
Pacific Time, my Mountain Time
beating against your Central Time, your
sun rising swiftly from the right my
sun rising swiftly from the left your
moon rising slowly from the left my
moon rising slowly from the right until
all four bodies of the sky
burn above us, sealing us together,
all our cities twin cities,
all our states united, one
nation, indivisible, with liberty and justice for all.

Like the Blowing of Birds' Eggs

Neil Rollinson

I crack the shell
on the bedstead and open it
over your stomach. It runs
to your navel and settles there
like the stone of a sharon fruit.

You ask me to gather it up
and pour it over your breast
without breaking the membrane.

It swims in my palm, drools
from the gaps in my fingers, fragrant,
spotted with blood.

It slips down your chest,
moves on your skin like a woman
hurrying in her yellow dress, the long
transparent train dragging behind.

It slides down your belly and into your
pubic hair where you burst
the yolk with a tap of your finger.

It covers your cunt in a shock
of gold. You tell me to eat,
to feel the sticky glair on my tongue.

I lick the folds of your sex, the coarse
damp hairs, the slopes of your arse
until you're clean, and tense as a clock spring.

I touch your spot and something inside you
explodes like the blowing of birds' eggs.

5

'But your wife said she'

The Faithful

Dan Burt

Will you reconnoitre after lunch,
Alone, mobile in hand for an urban
Nook from which to call where you
Will not be seen or heard, masking
Your aim like a jihadi, pleading
Exercise rather than Asr prayers?
If so, when you find a spot and press
The green key will blue paper catch
Sparking a blast across the sea?

Muslim martyrs are no different,
Dear, from you and me; sweet success
Will shatter both our worlds,
Though we may be more certain
Than they what our desserts will be.

The Sting

Patience Agbabi

At twelve I learnt about The Fall,
had rough-cut daydreams based on original sin,
nightmares about the swarm of thin-
lipped, foul-mouthed, crab apple-
masticating girls who'd chase me full
throttle: me, slipping on wet leaves, a heroine
in a black-and-white cliché; them, buzzing on nicotine
and the sap of French kisses. I hated big school
but even more, I hated the lurid shame
of surrender, the yellow miniskirt
my mother wore the day that that man
drove my dad's car to collect me. She called my name
softly, more seductive than an advert.
I heard the drone of the engine, turned and ran.

In the Victoria Hotel

John Saunders

I undress your innocence,
watched by the apostle of temperance
you kiss my lips, whisper – *this is us.*

We make love in the company of guilt,
shelter weakness in our hearts,
give safety to dangerous thoughts

and throw them to the pool of fate.
I believe every story it suggests,
dine on fine wines and purple dust.

This is the memory of our fading space,
a threadbare blanket of feeling –
every choice we make, a loss of freedom.

We dance in time to waltzes and tangos,
capture our history in mirrors of gold.

'For each ecstatic instant'

Emily Dickinson

For each ecstatic instant
We must an anguish pay
In keen and quivering ratio
To the ecstasy.

For each beloved hour
Sharp pittances of years,
Bitter contested farthings
And coffers heaped with tears.

'Doing, a filthy pleasure is, and short'

Gaius Petronius

Doing, a filthy pleasure is, and short;
And done, we straight repent us of the sport:
Let us not then rush blindly on unto it,
Like lustful beasts, that only know to do it:
For lust will languish, and that heat decay.
But thus, thus, keeping endless holiday,
Let us together closely lie and kiss,
There is no labour, nor no shame in this;
This hath pleased, doth please, and long will please; never
Can this decay, but is beginning ever.

Trans. Ben Jonson

The Marriage of Consonant and Vowel

Adam Horovitz

i

After the Wedding

Dreamt of you again last night,
your smiling face pushed close to mine;
caught between mirrors, a squeezebox
of repeats cluttering the line.

I thought as we were twitter-pressed
like sausage meat inside new skins
how little's known of what we love
hate and how compression bins

our excess dreams and sears off
the vowels of love; the consonants
of hurt are all that's left intact.
How does a lover thrive? Expanse!

No questing after jagged and reductive fact
but after puffball spores and seedlings of romance.

The Bride Has Taken the Vwls & Lft th Bldng

Drmt f y gn lst nt
yr :) pshd cls 2 mn;
cght btwn mrrrs, sqzbx
f rpts clttrng th ln.

Thght s w wr twttr-prssd
lke ssg mt nsd nw skns
hw lttl's knwn f wht w ♥
ht & hw cmprssn bns

r xs drms & srs ff
th vwls f ♥; th cnsnnts
f hrt r ll tht's lft ntct.
Hw ds lvr thrv? Xpns!

Nt qstng ftr jggd & rdctv fct
bt ftr pffbll sprs & sdlngs f rmnc.

The Bride in Her Lover's Bed

ea o ou aai a i,
ou ii ae ue oe o ie;
au eee io a ueeeo
o eea uei e ie.

i ou a e ee ie-ee
ie auae ea iie e i
o ie o o a e oe
ae a o oeio i

ou ee ea a ea o
e oe o oe e ooa
o u ae a a e ia.
o oe a oe ie? Eae!

o uei ae ae a euie a
u ae ua oe a eei o oae.

In Defence of Adultery

Julia Copus

We don't fall in love: it rises through us
the way that certain music does –
whether a symphony or ballad –
and it is sepia-coloured,
like spilt tea that inches up
the tiny tube-like gaps inside
a cube of sugar lying by a cup.
Yes, love's like that: just when we least
needed or expected it
a part of us dips into it
by chance or mishap and it seeps
through our capillaries, it clings
inside the chambers of the heart.
We're victims, we say: mere vessels,
drinking the vanilla scent
of this one's skin, the lustre
of another's eyes so skilfully
darkened with bistre. And whatever
damage might result we're not
to blame for it: love is an autocrat
and won't be disobeyed.
Sometimes we manage
to convince ourselves of that.

Office Friendships

Gavin Ewart

Eve is madly in love with Hugh
And Hugh is keen on Jim.
Charles is in love with very few
And few are in love with him.

Myra sits typing notes of love
With romantic pianist's fingers.
Dick turns his eyes to the heavens above
Where Fran's divine perfume lingers.

Nicky is rolling eyes and tits
And flaunting her wiggly walk.
Everybody is thrilled to bits
By Clive's suggestive talk.

Sex suppressed will go berserk,
But it keeps us all alive.
It's a wonderful change from wives and work
And it ends at half past five.

Her News

Hugo Williams

You paused for a moment and I heard you smoking
on the other end of the line.
I pictured your expression,
one eye screwed shut against the smoke
as you waited for my reaction.
I was waiting for it myself, a list of my own news
gone suddenly cold in my hand.
Supposing my wife found out, what would happen then?
Would I have to leave her and marry you now?
Perhaps it wouldn't be so bad,
starting again with someone new, finding a new place,
pretending the best was yet to come.
It might even be fun,
playing the family man, walking around in the park
full of righteous indignation.
But no, I couldn't go through all that again,
not without my own wife being there,
not without her getting cross about everything.
Perhaps she wouldn't mind about the baby,
then we could buy a house in the country
and all move in together.
That sounded like a better idea.
Now that I'd been caught at last, a wave of relief
swept over me. I was just considering
a shed in the garden with a radio and a day bed,
when I remembered I hadn't seen you for over a year.
'Congratulations,' I said. 'When's it due?'

Story of a Hotel Room

Rosemary Tonks

Thinking we were safe – insanity!
We went in to make love. All the same
Idiots to trust the little hotel bedroom
Then in the gloom . . .
. . . And who does not know that pair of shutters
With the awkward hook on them
All screeching whispers? Very well then, in the gloom
We set about acquiring one another
Urgently! But on a temporary basis
Only as guests – just guests of one another's senses.

But idiots to feel so safe you hold back nothing
Because the bed of cold, electric linen
Happens to be illicit . . .
To make love as well as that is ruinous.
Londoner, Parisian, someone should have warned us
That without permanent intentions
You have absolutely no protection –
If the act is clean, authentic, sumptuous,
The concurring deep love of the heart
Follows the naked work, profoundly moved by it.

may i feel

e. e. cummings

may i feel said he
(i'll squeal said she
just once said he)
it's fun said she

(may i touch said he
how much said she
a lot said he)
why not said she

(let's go said he
not too far said she
what's too far said he
where you are said she)

may i stay said he
(which way said she
like this said he
if you kiss said she

may i move said he
is it love said she)
if you're willing said he
(but you're killing said she

but it's life said he
but your wife said she
now said he)
ow said she

(tiptop said he
don't stop said she
oh no said he)
go slow said she

(cccome? said he
ummm said she)
you're divine! said he
(you are Mine said she)

Adultery

Carol Ann Duffy

Wear dark glasses in the rain.
Regard what was unhurt
as though through a bruise.
Guilt. A sick, green tint.

New gloves, money tucked in the palms,
the handshake crackles. Hands
can do many things. Phone.
Open the wine. Wash themselves. Now

you are naked under your clothes all day,
slim with deceit. Only the once
brings you alone to your knees,
miming, more, more, older and sadder,

creative. Suck a lie with a hole in it
on the way home from a lethal, thrilling night
up against a wall, faster. Language
unpeels a lost cry. You're a bastard.

Do it do it do it. Sweet darkness
in the afternoon; a voice in your ear
telling you how you are wanted,
which way, now. A telltale clock

wiping the hours from its face, your face
on a white sheet, gasping, radiant, yes.
Pay for it in cash, fiction, cab-fares back
to the life which crumbles like a wedding-cake.

Paranoia for lunch; too much
to drink, as a hand on your thigh
tilts the restaurant. You know all about love,
don't you. Turn on your beautiful eyes

for a stranger who's dynamite in bed, again
and again; a slow replay in the kitchen
where the slicing of innocent onions
scalds you to tears. Then, selfish autobiographical sleep

in a marital bed, the tarnished spoon of your body
stirring betrayal, your heart over-ripe at the core.
You're an expert, darling; your flowers
dumb and explicit on nobody's birthday.

So write the script – illness and debt,
a ring thrown away in a garden
no moon can heal, your own words
commuting to bile in your mouth, terror –

and all for the same thing twice. And all
for the same thing twice. You did it.
What. Didn't you. Fuck. Fuck. No. That was
the wrong verb. This is only an abstract noun.

The Dark Night of the Sole

Kit Wright

'My husband's an odd fish,' she said.
  A casual remark
And yet it lingered in my head
And later, when we went to bed,
  It woke me in the dark.

My husband's an odd fish. I lay
  Uneasy. On the ceiling
Raw lorry lights strobe-lit the grey
Glimmer of dawn. Sleepless dismay
  Revolved upon the feeling

Of something wrong in what I'd heard,
  Some deep, unhappy thing,
Some *odder* fact her statement blurred.
And then a prickling horror stirred
  Within me as the wing

Of madness brushed. I recognized
  The real thing strange to be
Not dorsal structure (fins disguised)
Nor travel habits (route revised:
  A Day Return to sea)

But that he was a fish at all!
  Trembling, I left the bed
Dressed quickly, tiptoed through the hall,
Edged past him, gaping from his stall
  Of oval water, fled

To where I sit and write these lines,
  Sweating. I saw and heard
Strange things last night. Cold guilt defines
The moral: learn to read the signs –
  She was an odd, odd bird.

'The expense of spirit in a waste of shame'

William Shakespeare

The expense of spirit in a waste of shame
Is lust in action: and till action, lust
Is perjur'd, murderous, bloody, full of blame,
Savage, extreme, rude, cruel, not to trust;
Enjoy'd no sooner but despised straight;
Past reason hunted; and no sooner had,
Past reason hated, as a swallow'd bait,
On purpose laid to make the taker mad:
Mad in pursuit and in possession so;
Had, having, and in quest to have, extreme;
A bliss in proof, – and prov'd, a very woe;
Before, a joy propos'd; behind a dream.
All this the world well knows; yet none knows well
To shun the heaven that leads men to this hell.

Cyber Infidelity

Jane Holland

Beautiful lover, still beautiful
because unseen, as far apart

as two incalculable griefs
on either side of a war, cast

the broken parts of yourself
over the bridge that separates us –

no less incomprehensible
than history back into the void

where a limp, or squint, halitosis,
puckered rolls of flesh, a voice

abrupt as a bedspring, can be shed
for this dazzling dive naked

into a fast-as-light vernacular,
cunnilingus of the internet,

fellatio of different parts
of speech – delete, delete, amend –

while the caches of the fluttering ghosts
of our other halves, asleep in bed,

send silent cookies to the heart:
bedtime now, put out the light.

To His Lost Lover

Simon Armitage

Now they are no longer
any trouble to each other

he can turn things over, get down to that list
of things that never happened, all of the lost

unfinishable business.
For instance . . . for instance,

how he never clipped and kept her hair, or drew a hairbrush
through that style of hers, and never knew how not to blush

at the fall of her name in close company.
How they never slept like buried cutlery –

two spoons or forks cupped perfectly together,
or made the most of some heavy weather –

walked out into hard rain under sheet lightning,
or did the gears while the other was driving.

How he never raised his fingertips
to stop the segments of her lips

from breaking the news,
or tasted the fruit

or picked for himself the pear of her heart,
or lifted her hand to where his own heart

was a small, dark, terrified bird
in her grip. Where it hurt.

Or said the right thing,
or put it in writing.

And never fled the black mile back to his house
before midnight, or coaxed another button of her blouse,

then another,
or knew her

favourite colour,
her taste, her flavour,

and never ran a bath or held a towel for her,
or soft-soaped her, or whipped her hair

into an ice-cream cornet or a beehive
of lather, or acted out of turn, or misbehaved

when he might have, or worked a comb
where no comb had been, or walked back home

through a black mile hugging a punctured heart,
where it hurt, where it hurt, or helped her hand

to his butterfly heart
in its two blue halves.

And never almost cried,
and never once described

an attack of the heart,
or under a silk shirt

nursed in his hand her breast,
her left, like a tear of flesh

wept by the heart,
where it hurts,

or brushed with his thumb the nut of her nipple,
or drank intoxicating liquors from her navel.

Or christened the Pole Star in her name,
or shielded the mask of her face like a flame,

a pilot light,
or stayed the night,

or steered her back to that house of his,
or said 'Don't ask me how it is

I like you.
I just might do.'

How he never figured out a fireproof plan,
or unravelled her hand, as if her hand

were a solid ball
of silver foil

and discovered a lifeline hiding inside it,
and measured the trace of his own alongside it.

But said some things and never meant them –
sweet nothings anybody could have mentioned.

And left unsaid some things he should have spoken,
about the heart, where it hurt exactly, and how often.

Ending

Gavin Ewart

The love we thought would never stop
now cools like a congealing chop.
The kisses that were hot as curry
are bird-pecks taken in a hurry.
The hands that held electric charges
now lie inert as four moored barges.
The feet that ran to meet a date
are running slow and running late.
The eyes that shone and seldom shut
are victims of a power cut.
The parts that then transmitted joy
are now reserved and cold and coy.
Romance, expected once to stay,
has left a note saying GONE AWAY.

Rubbish at Adultery

Sophie Hannah

Must I give up another night
To hear you whinge and whine
About how terribly grim you feel
And what a dreadful swine
You are? You say you'll never leave
Your wife and children. Fine;

When have I ever asked you to?
I'd settle for a kiss.
Couldn't you, for an hour or so,
Just leave them out of *this*?
A rare ten minutes off from guilty
Diatribes – what bliss.

Yes, I'm aware you're sensitive:
A tortured, wounded soul.
I'm after passion, thrills, and fun.
You say fun takes its toll,
So what are we doing here? I fear
We've lost our common goal.

You're rubbish at adultery.
I think you ought to quit.
Trouble is, at fidelity,
You're also slightly shit.
Choose one and do it properly
You stupid, stupid git.

End of the Affair

Dan Burt

It ends soundlessly: my hand slips yours
To adjust demeanour for a neighbour,
No bang, bombed body sprawled, no prayer,
Just a gentle unlacing of fingers
Wrests warp from woof in the tapestry we
Fashioned from Fragonards and poetry
To decorate our idyll. We stand
Naked by the roadside with vagrant hands,
Sunlit in senescent imperfection,
My stoop and vanished waist, runt canyons
Time and disappointment wore in your face,
In silence that surrounds a fall from grace
And separate soon after, sans goodbye,
Relieved what never lived had died.

6

'What's in it for me?'

Badly Chosen Lover

Rosemary Tonks

Criminal, you took a great piece of my life,
And you took it under false pretences,
That piece of time
– In the clear muscles of my brain
I have the lens and jug of it!
Books, thoughts, meals, days, and houses,
Half Europe, spent like a coarse banknote,
You took it – leaving mud and cabbage stumps.

And, Criminal, I damn you for it (very softly).
My spirit broke her fast on you. And, Turk,
You fed her with the breath of your neck
– In my brain's clear retina
I have the stolen love-behaviour.
Your heart, greedy and tepid, brothel-meat,
Gulped it like a flunkey with erotica.
And very softly, Criminal, I damn you for it.

Fetish

Samantha Willis

I can see this relationship tanking,
so it's time to be honest, I think.
In the space between dreaming and wanking,
I've developed a striking new kink.

Though I used to be coy and coquettish,
as all men like their women to be,
my new-leaf aspirational fetish
is demanding, 'What's in it for me?'

I can see this might be disconcerting
for a man who likes hookers and porn,
in whose mind every female is squirting
to the sound of his name, dusk till dawn,

so let's get you some sex education
with incentives: my Love USP
is undying devout adoration
but first tell me: what's in it for me?

You would like me to make you my hero,
to discuss, at great length, Aston Villa;
in exchange you are offering zero;
one-way traffic. So dull. So vanilla.

I'll forgive your flawed pacing (too snaily);
I'll provide all you need, and for free,
and I'm happy to email you daily
if you tell me what's in it for me.

Is it something I'm presently lacking?
A locked room with an out-of-reach key?
If you want my support and my backing
then I think anyone would agree
you must tell me what's in it for me.

Please, before I'm a hundred and three,
can you tell me what's in it for me?

From Strugnell's Sonnets

Wendy Cope

The expense of spirits is a crying shame,
So is the cost of wine. What bard today
Can live like old Khayyam? It's not the same –
A loaf and Thou and Tesco's Beaujolais.
I had this bird called Sharon. Fond of gin –
Could knock back six or seven. At the price
I paid a high wage for each hour of sin
And that was why I only had her twice.
Then there was Tracy, who drank rum and Coke.
So beautiful I didn't mind at first
But love grows colder. Now some other bloke
Is subsidizing Tracy and her thirst.
I need a woman, honest and sincere,
Who'll come across on half a pint of beer.

Message

Wendy Cope

Pick up the phone before it is too late
And dial my number. There's no time to spare –
Love is already turning into hate
And very soon I'll start to look elsewhere.

Good, old-fashioned men like you are rare –
You want to get to know me at a rate
That's guaranteed to drive me to despair.
Pick up the phone before it is too late.

Well, wouldn't it be nice to consummate
Our friendship while we've still got teeth and hair?
Just bear in mind that you are forty-eight
And dial my number. There's no time to spare.

Another kamikaze love affair?
No chance. This time I'll have to learn to wait
But one more day is more than I can bear –
Love is already turning into hate.

Of course, my friends say I exaggerate
And dramatize a lot. That may be fair
But it is no fun being in this state
And very soon I'll start to look elsewhere.

I know you like me but I wouldn't dare
Ring you again. Instead I'll concentrate
On sending thought-waves through the London air
And, if they reach you, please don't hesitate –
Pick up the phone.

Benny Hill

Paul McGrane

This bloke is sitting on a bus
We cut to where a sign says PUSH
beneath a bell the bell is pushed
We cut again Outside a caff
the door says PULL he pulls the door
Inside the caff the waitress comes
of course she's young and beautiful
We have a close up on his face
He rolls his eyes and licks his lips
and reaches out toward her chest
her badge says PAT he pats the badge

Your face looked like that actresses'
when you caught me with your sister
at the party in her bedroom
we were dancing to old records
we'd speeded up to 45
so they would sound like Benny Hill
I've changed the ending of this scene
to make it seem more humorous
You're chasing me through parks and fields
dressed in heels and red suspenders
mock-angry fist raised in the air
And me? I'm Benny Hill! At last!
With no responsibilities
except for making people laugh
and grabbing their extremities

Anal Obsessive

Jane Holland

He was a blip on the radar – I had
several that year – but since
he was up front about it –
'Don't trust me, I'm a bastard' –
I let him screw me, and then
screw me. The woman
he left me for was older,
uncompromising, sober.
She would never have rolled over
for that sharp pain
in the derriere, or thought
extensively of England,
face pressed into his mattress
with its bachelor stains
and cute ringlets of pubic hair.
I remember his stubble,
the wind-tunnel tilt of his penis,
how I stripped off for him
the way it's done in Amsterdam –
to be greased up, pokered
and prodded – and can't
imagine now why I bothered.

Katya is Bored

Fiona Pitt-Kethley

Katya is bored – as bored as I would be
if I perused a sack of Blyton books.
Katya has worked the Tanga Club for years,
in Grosse Freiheit off the Reeperbahn.
Her Chilean partner looks a little bored,
though he's not half as bored as Katya is.
Above, below, behind, legs up, legs down . . .
The fucks clock up . . .The audience loses count.

Katya is bored. She's far too bored to act.
The corners of her mouth turn firmly down.
Her eyes stare firmly at the scene ahead,
locked on to nothing, somewhere in our midst.
She's shagged and doggy-fucked around the club,
on drinkers' tables, floors, the bars, a swing.

Can endless repetition bore to death?
If boredom was a terminal disease,
She's long gone dead. Bored fucking, fucking bored.
The monumental ennui she exudes
each time her partner's plunger plumbs her sink
impresses me. She makes no compromise.
She has a rule. She never smiles at work.

Chris of Dublin

Fiona Pitt-Kethley

A brothel with a creche for the girls' kids,
long gone now and it is a darker scene,
no help for those who choose to walk the streets.
I met Chris, young and bruised, with missing teeth,
and drunk, and heard her history of abuse,
abuse that no-one ever had believed.
My courage faltered. Back in my hotel
a wave of fear swept through me to my soul.
I pushed a cabinet against my door.
Thus shutting out the darkness of outside,
lives without hope, torture, torment, abuse.
I slept and woke to write her story up.
I wish her well, wherever she is now.
Somehow I doubt that Chris is still alive.

Jaffa Cakes

Fiona Pitt-Kethley

Three neon strips, one violet and two red,
mark out the bars that really are not bars.
Girls from Zaire, who're tall and elegant,
and Belgian blondes sit in red fun fur chairs
or pose with stomachs in, tits out on stools.
The windows where girls sit are full of props.
Some girls are reading. Others do their nails.
Yet others gorge themselves on takeaways.
When clients come they disappear from view.
I studied the windows when I couldn't catch their eye,
looked at what's left behind: their lingerie,
brushes for make-up, mirrors and high heels.
One window's different from the rest of them,
a Buddha statue and some Jaffa cakes.

I told this story to a Polish friend.
He said he'd definitely visit there.
Couldn't resist a brothel with Jaffa cakes.

Buggery

Don Paterson

At round about four months or so –
the time is getting shorter –
I look down as the face below
goes sliding underwater

and though I know it's over with
and she is miles from me
I stay a while to mine the earth
For what was lost at sea

as if the faces of the drowned
might turn up in the harrow;
hold me while I hold you down
and plough the lonely furrow

Carmen 16

Gaius Valerius Catullus

I'll fuck your ass and rape your face
Cock-gobbling, power-bottom poets
Who say my fancy, fluffy measures
Make me a flaccid, fluffing fag.
A pious poet should be pure
But his poems don't have to be.
Poetry should taste like sex.
Its meaty words can lick and flit
Their tongues to scratch the itch that lifts
Not just young boys but wrinkled men
Whose cocks are as curdled as their lines.
Because you've read my kissing poems
You think you can make my mouth your cunt?
I'll fuck your ass and rape your face!

Trans. G. M. Palmer

To His Coy Mistress

Andrew Marvell

Had we but world enough, and time,
This coyness, Lady, were no crime.
We would sit down and think which way
To walk and pass our long love's day.
Thou by the Indian Ganges' side
Shouldst rubies find: I by the tide
Of Humber would complain. I would
Love you ten years before the Flood,
And you should, if you please, refuse
Till the conversion of the Jews.
My vegetable love should grow
Vaster than empires, and more slow;
An hundred years should go to praise
Thine eyes and on thy forehead gaze;
Two hundred to adore each breast;
But thirty thousand to the rest;
An age at least to every part,
And the last age should show your heart;
For, Lady, you deserve this state,
Nor would I love at lower rate.
   But at my back I always hear
Time's wingèd chariot hurrying near;
And yonder all before us lie
Deserts of vast eternity.
Thy beauty shall no more be found,
Nor, in thy marble vault, shall sound
My echoing song: then worms shall try
That long preserved virginity,
And your quaint honour turn to dust,

And into ashes all my lust:
The grave's a fine and private place,
But none, I think, do there embrace.
　　Now therefore, while the youthful hue
Sits on thy skin like morning dew,
And while thy willing soul transpires
At every pore with instant fires,
Now let us sport us while we may,
And now, like amorous birds of prey,
Rather at once our time devour
Than languish in his slow-chapt power.
Let us roll all our strength and all
Our sweetness up into one ball,
And tear our pleasures with rough strife
Through the iron gates of life:
Thus, though we cannot make our sun
Stand still, yet we will make him run.

The Flea

John Donne

Mark but this flea, and mark in this,
How little that which thou deniest me is;
It sucked me first, and now sucks thee,
And in this flea our two bloods mingled be;
Thou know'st that this cannot be said
A sin, nor shame, nor loss of maidenhead,
   Yet this enjoys before it woo,
    And pampered swells with one blood made of two,
    And this, alas, is more than we would do.

Oh stay, three lives in one flea spare,
Where we almost, nay more than married are.
This flea is you and I, and this
Our marriage bed, and marriage temple is;
Though parents grudge, and you, w'are met,
And cloistered in these living walls of jet.
   Though use make you apt to kill me,
    Let not to that, self-murder added be,
    And sacrilege, three sins in killing three.

Cruel and sudden, hast thou since
Purpled thy nail, in blood of innocence?
Wherein could this flea guilty be,
Except in that drop which it sucked from thee?
Yet thou triumph'st, and say'st that thou
Find'st not thy self, nor me the weaker now;
   'Tis true; then learn how false, fears be:
    Just so much honor, when thou yield'st to me,
    Will waste, as this flea's death took life from thee.

Hombres Necios

Sor Juana Inés de la Cruz

Hombres necios que acusáis
a la mujer sin razón,
sin ver que sois la ocasión
de lo mismo que culpáis:

si con ansia sin igual
solicitáis su desdén,
¿por qué quereis que obren bien
si las incitáis al mal?

Combatís su resistencia
y luego, con gravedad,
decís que fue liviandad
lo que hizo la diligencia.

Parecer quiere el denuedo
de vuestro parecer loco,
al niño que pone el coco
y luego le tiene miedo.

Queréis, con presunción necia,
hallar a la que buscáis,
para pretendida, Thais,
y en la posesión, Lucrecia

¿Qué humor puede ser más raro
que el que, falto de consejo,
el mismo empaña el espejo
y siente que no esté claro?

Con el favor y el desdén
tenéis condición igual,
quejándoos, si os tratan mal,
burlándoos, si os quieren bien.

Opinión, ninguna gana:
pues la que más se recata,
si no os admite, es ingrata,
y si os admite, es liviana

Siempre tan necios andáis
que, con desigual nivel,
a una culpáis por crüel
y a otra por fácil culpáis.

¿Pues cómo ha de estar templada
la que vuestro amor pretende,
si la que es ingrata, ofende,
y la que es fácil, enfada?

Mas, entre el enfado y pena
que vuestro gusto refiere,
bien haya la que no os quiere
y quejaos en hora buena.

Dan vuestras amantes penas
a sus libertades alas,
y después de hacerlas malas
las queréis hallar muy buenas.

¿Cuál mayor culpa ha tenido
en una pasión errada:
la que cae de rogada
o el que ruega de caído?

¿O cuál es más de culpar,
aunque cualquiera mal haga:
la que peca por la paga
o el que paga por pecar?

Pues ¿para quée os espantáis
de la culpa que tenéis?
Queredlas cual las hacéis
o hacedlas cual las buscáis.

Dejad de solicitar,
y después, con más razón,
acusaréis la afición
de la que os fuere a rogar.

Bien con muchas armas fundo
que lidia vuestra arrogancia,
pues en promesa e instancia
juntáis diablo, carne y mundo.

Stupid Men

Silly, you men – so very adept
at wrongly faulting womankind,
not seeing you're alone to blame
for faults you plant in woman's mind.

After you've won by urgent plea
the right to tarnish her good name,
you still expect her to behave –
you, that coaxed her into shame.

You batter her resistance down
and then, all righteousness, proclaim
that feminine frivolity,
not your persistence, is to blame.

When it comes to bravely posturing,
your witlessness must take the prize:
you're the child that makes a bogeyman,
and then recoils in fear and cries.

Presumptuous beyond belief,
you'd have the woman you pursue
be Thais when you're courting her,
Lucretia once she falls to you.

For plain default of common sense,
could any action be so queer
as oneself to cloud the mirror,
then complain that it's not clear?

Whether you're favoured or disdained,
nothing can leave you satisfied.
You whimper if you're turned away,
you sneer if you've been gratified.

With you, no woman can hope to score;
whichever way, she's bound to lose;
spurning you, she's ungrateful –
succumbing, you call her lewd.

Your folly is always the same:
you apply a single rule
to the one you accuse of looseness
and the one you brand as cruel.

What happy mean could there be
for the woman who catches your eye,
if, unresponsive, she offends,
yet whose complaisance you decry?

Still, whether it's torment or anger –
and both ways you've yourselves to blame –
God bless the woman who won't have you,
no matter how loud you complain.

It's your persistent entreaties
that change her from timid to bold.
Having made her thereby naughty,
you would have her good as gold.

So where does the greater guilt lie
for a passion that should not be:
with the man who pleads out of baseness
or the woman debased by his plea?

Or which is more to be blamed –
though both will have cause for chagrin:
the woman who sins for money
or the man who pays money to sin?

So why are you men all so stunned
at the thought you're all guilty alike?
Either like them for what you've made them
or make of them what you can like.

If you'd give up pursuing them,
you'd discover, without a doubt,
you've a stronger case to make
against those who seek you out.

I well know what powerful arms
you wield in pressing for evil:
your arrogance is allied
with the world, the flesh, and the devil!

Ego

Eileen Sheehan

When she doesn't want to make love
he says, *What's wrong?*
As if something must be.

She says, *There's nothing wrong.*

He says, *But there must be something wrong.*
The master, needing reasons.

She feels she should
have a note from her mother . . .

Dear Sir
would you please excuse my daughter from sex
the time of the month is not right
she's worried about the telephone bill
an earthquake rocked Tokyo tonight
she's afraid of waking the baby
Halley's comet won't pass again for sixty-seven years
she's afraid of making a baby
and the Dow Jones index showed
an unfavourable low at close of business
and you probably did it last night
two nights ago at the most . . .

He nudges her with his elbow.
Go on, you can tell me what's wrong.
Was it something I did? Something I said?

But there's nothing wrong, I keep telling you!

Deflated, he heaves towards the wall,
taking his questions, and most of the blankets.

Freezing on the edge of the world
she knows that nothing is wrong,
for tonight she has learnt three things;

about ego,
the tug of the moon,
why women invented the headache.

Annus Mirabilis

Philip Larkin

Sexual intercourse began
In nineteen sixty-three
(which was rather late for me) –
Between the end of the *Chatterley* ban
And the Beatles' first LP.

Up to then there'd only been
A sort of bargaining,
A wrangle for the ring,
A shame that started at sixteen
And spread to everything.

Then all at once the quarrel sank:
Everyone felt the same,
And every life became
A brilliant breaking of the bank,
A quite unlosable game.

So life was never better than
In nineteen sixty-three
(Though just too late for me) –
Between the end of the *Chatterley* ban
And the Beatles' first LP.

7

'Oh right. You people don't remove that bit'

Bloody Hell, It's Barbara!

Luke Wright

The tits that crashed a thousand cars,
a hot knife through the city's bars,
full complement of facial scars –
Bloody hell, it's Barbara!

All thunder thighs and lightning hair,
resplendent in her underwear,
I want that one, it isn't fair!
Bloody hell, it's Barbara!

Well versed in dark romantic arts,
she feeds each night on fledgling hearts,
indeed on any private parts –
Bloody hell, it's Barbara!

Bloody hell! OMG! *Sacré bleu!* It's Barbara!
As sumptuous and stylish as a Gothic candelabra.
I want to dock my dinghy in the safety of your harbour.
A bidet full of ice would not begin to cool my ardour.

The kind of broad that gangsters rate,
the type to make kings abdicate,
enough to turn the Navy straight –
Bloody hell, it's Barbara!

Boudicca but soaked in liquor,
tactless as a bumper sticker,
Oh la la, my dicker ticker!
Bloody hell, it's Barbara!

Think boozy busty nightclub rep
meets Super Nanny all windswept,
I think I need the naughty step –
Bloody hell, it's Barbara!

Bloody hell! What's all this? Free Tibet! It's Barbara.
Imagine Mrs Robinson, if she had come from Scarborough.
She twists herself around you like clematis on an arbour.
In every English town a fella's weeping to his barber.
Bloody hell, it's Barbara!
Bloody hell, it's Barbara!

Her love is aching arteries,
her night caps nips of anti-freeze,
my sonnets bawdy journalese,
as sure as pepper makes you sneeze
and Russians come from overseas,
I want you Barbara, can I please,
I need to hear you pant and wheeze,
I'm begging you, I'm on my knees,
just give me all your STDs –
Bloody hell, it's Barbara!

Bloody hell! Stop the clocks! Bring out your dead! It's Barbara.
I want to take a tit-bit from your cool and gloomy larder.
I think I'm at the end now 'cause the rhymes are getting harder,
so here it is, the chorus line
just shout it out one final time –
Bloody hell, it's Barbara!

Sex without Love

Sharon Olds

How do they do it, the ones who make love
without love? Beautiful as dancers,
gliding over each other like ice-skaters
over the ice, fingers hooked
inside each other's bodies, faces
red as steak, wine, wet as the
children at birth whose mothers are going to
give them away. How do they come to the
come to the come to the God come to the
still waters, and not love
the one who came there with them, light
rising slowly as steam off their joined
skin? These are the true religious,
the purists, the pros, the ones who will not
accept a false Messiah, love the
priest instead of the God. They do not
mistake the lover for their own pleasure,
they are like great runners: they know they are alone
with the road surface, the cold, the wind,
the fit of their shoes, their over-all cardio-
vascular health – just factors, like the partner
in the bed, and not the truth, which is the
single body alone in the universe
against its own best time.

Out of Office

Cora Greenhill

Just after the interview, he'd groped
her breasts inside her low cut dress.
She didn't resist. And so it went on.
Disarmed by his cool persistence,
she agreed to this tryst in town.
The Mercedes had deep leather seats
and tinted windows, dimming her view
of the naked women washing in ditches
along the road to Enugu.

The narrow room was stifling hot
in the afternoon. The Professor,
so charming, so well-read, sweated
as he slurped his bush meat soup,
sat beside her on the single bed.
She'd asked for a club sandwich and coke
but it hadn't come and nothing was said.

He wiped his mouth, removed her dress,
arranged her like books on his desk,
Scanning her nakedness like a good report,
he straddled her, unbuttoned, taut.
But when his hand rubbed up against
her swollen shaft, a gasp, 'What's that?'
Then, proud of recalling the quirky fact,
'Oh right. You people don't remove that bit,
isn't it?'

Somehow she let him carry on –
sawing away like a carpenter
while she grew wet and sore
and didn't come. Straight after, he said
he had to get home to pick up his mum.
The mother didn't stoop to greet her,
in the back of the car where he'd left her
– just a new white assistant teacher.

Poem while Reading Miroslav Holub in the Genito-urinary Clinic Waiting Room

Rich Goodson

Live, alive-ho! These bugs! These bugs! Alive!
They've leapt between us since we flapped in slime,
jump ship, like pirates, to the brink of Time.
We're hit. We take in water. They survive.

& here we wait for test results, pretend
to read. You: *What Car?* Me: Holub's *Selected*
which permeates my bones till I'm infected.

Does every rhyme of loins sound out the end?

If you weren't such a bloke I'd hold your hand
uncurl it, break it open like a tight
wet waterlily bulb, there to find – stowed –
the toxic larvae of angels. I'd wind
the clocks back to that hot, barbaric night.
I'd burn them off your palm, watch them explode.

King Solomon and King David

James Ball Naylor

King Solomon and King David
Led merry merry lives
With many many lady friends
And many many wives;
But when old age crept up on them
With many many qualms,
King Solomon wrote the Proverbs
And King David wrote the Psalms.

The Walk of Shame

Nikki Magennis

Last night's gladrags transform in daylight.
Crimson lipstick bitten from the very centre
of my mouth leaves a tide line, heart shaped.

These red shoes were never meant for treading
the long path home – kitten heels jack me up
pointing sinwards, downhill as fast as I

can possibly slide. The holes snagged in my tights gape
wide as the mouth of a shocked onlooker, as if your hands
had left prints in a repeating pattern

all over my lower half. Can they tell,
the street sweepers, delivery men and dirty-faced tramps
that I've been out all night, mauling hot flesh

getting intimate with an unknown lover?
This morning I walk home empty handed
nameless, and despite myself, carrying no trace of regret.

Municipal Ambition

Amy McCauley

When I think of the bodies I ran from.
Throwing myself on the mercy of grass pastures and filthy
   mattresses.
The springs, the bedsits, the landscape miniatures.
And worst of all, the way they sewed me up like a purse
so I wouldn't try and get out.
Or in, they couldn't decide which.

When I think of the bad love.
The girl who lost it again and again on that patch of municipal
   lawn.
Hot sap running down her thighs.
The girl who held herself at arm's length all her life.
Who couldn't bear to look herself in the eye
let alone love.

When I think of the neglect.
The years of untended want gone to waste.
My God. I could go down on my knees and weep.
Weep! like a silent movie heroine bathed in the torchlight of pathos.
And all my starved orifices would form a chorus of sobs
and pourforth, sputtering like outside taps.

When I think of the pangs in windowless rooms.
The years of skulduggery and subterfuge.
I could swear it was someone else the whole time.
I could scream:
Make way for more!
More bad love! More neglect! More pourforth!

Madmen

Fleur Adcock

Odd how the seemingly maddest of men –
sheer loonies, the classically paranoid
violently possessive about their secrets,
whispered after from corners, terrified
of poison in their coffee, driven frantic
(whether for or against him) by discussion of God
peculiar, to say the least, about their mothers –
return to their gentle senses in bed.

Suddenly straightforward, they perform
with routine confidence, neither afraid
that their partner will turn and bite their balls off
nor groping under the pillow for a razor blade;
eccentric only in their conversation,
which rambles on about the meaning of a word
they used in an argument in 1969,
they leave their women grateful, relieved, and bored.

Can Clio Do More than Amuse?
(after Verlaine)

Eva Salzman

My lovers are not literary types.
They are labourers on building sites.
They build houses and dig drains.
They do not sip champagne.

I want their strong arms to pin me to the bed.
I want them to enjoy me without romance,
simply, the way they take their beer and bread.
I want to make them hard and make them dance.

They do not own a tie or fancy shirts,
or a single suit. Their bodies have an earthy scent
or reek of cheap cologne like Brut.
Their hands are rough and thick, and elegant.

They're not so hot at grammar, except in bed
where suddenly every word they say is correctly said.
They may not wash sometimes, but breathe me in
as if my skin were made of oxygen.

They trail a tang of sweat and stale tobacco everywhere.
Unfinished at the edges, they don't wear underwear.
All they do is belch and fuck and hawk and fart.
They can't tell the difference between their prick and their heart.

The Final Coming

Irving Layton

Her lips were round and full
And to his lap she bent;
He saw no car ahead
And when he came he went.

8

'God, to be wanted once more'

To the Virgins, to Make Much of Time

Robert Herrick

Gather ye rosebuds while ye may,
Old Time is still a-flying;
And this same flower that smiles today
Tomorrow will be dying.

The glorious lamp of heaven, the sun,
The higher he's a-getting,
The sooner will his race be run,
And nearer he's to setting.

That age is best which is the first,
When youth and blood are warmer;
But being spent, the worse, and worst
Times still succeed the former.

Then be not coy, but use your time,
And while ye may, go marry;
For having lost but once your prime,
You may forever tarry.

One Flesh

Elizabeth Jennings

Lying apart now, each in a separate bed,
He with a book, keeping the light on late,
She like a girl dreaming of childhood,
All men elsewhere – it is as if they wait
Some new event: the book he holds unread,
Her eyes fixed on the shadows overhead.

Tossed up like flotsam from a former passion,
How cool they lie. They hardly ever touch,
Or if they do, it is like a confession
Of having little feeling – or too much.
Chastity faces them, a destination
For which their whole lives were a preparation.

Strangely apart, yet strangely close together,
Silence between them like a thread to hold
And not wind in. And time itself's a feather
Touching them gently. Do they know they're old,
These two who are my father and my mother
Whose fire from which I came, has now grown cold?

To Her Ancient Lover

John Wilmot, Earl of Rochester

Ancient person, for whom I,
All the flattering youth defy;
Long be it e'er thou grow old,
Aching, shaking, crazy cold.
But still continue as thou art,
Ancient person of my heart.

On thy withered lips and dry,
Which like barren furrows lye;
Brooding kisses I will pour,
Shall thy youthful heat restore.
Such kind showers in autumn fall,
And a second spring recall:
Nor from thee will ever part,
Ancient person of my heart.

Thy nobler part, which but to name
In our sex would be counted shame,
By age's frozen grasp possessed,
From his ice shall be released,
And soothed by my reviving hand,
In former warmth and vigour stand.
All a lover's wish can reach,
For thy joy my love shall teach;
And for thy pleasure shall improve,
All that art can add to love.
Yet still I love thee without art,
Ancient person of my heart.

Address

C. H. Sisson

You whom I never loved,
You I have never touched
Live in my mind as if you proved
A thesis about other such,

Which is, that firm and tender flesh
Is medicine for an ageing man,
As if one body could refresh
Another as it never can.

The crook of age, the spring of youth,
Are equally the work of time;
What is in common is the truth
That age is age and prime is prime

And that both quickly slip away
To other hours, or none at all:
Whatever words the ghosts may say
It is the bodies take the fall.

Pretence may entertain the old,
The young may answer with a lie
But neither old nor young can hold
The same illusion till they die.

I look on you, you look on me;
For both, to speak no word is best.
I contemplate your lovely youth;
You cannot bear to think the rest.

'What lips my lips have kissed, and where, and why'

Edna St Vincent Millay

What lips my lips have kissed, and where, and why,
I have forgotten, and what arms have lain
Under my head till morning; but the rain
Is full of ghosts tonight, that tap and sigh
Upon the glass and listen for reply,
And in my heart there stirs a quiet pain
For unremembered lads that not again
Will turn to me at midnight with a cry.
Thus in winter stands the lonely tree,
Nor knows what birds have vanished one by one,
Yet knows its boughs more silent than before:
I cannot say what loves have come and gone,
I only know that summer sang in me
A little while, that in me sings no more.

On the French Riviera

Ian Pindar

Youth and beauty have left me
   a full packet of cigarettes
and this balcony. Time redecorates
   my home as a reliquary.

The camera loved me once,
   as everyone loves a young woman
of spirit who toys with men
   and uses her natural elegance

to get what she wants. Siren
   or ingénue, whatever they asked of me
I exuded 'a carefree, naive sexuality',
   the critics said. Dominique, is that Dorian

at the door? My official biographer
   promised to swing by after church
with more questions. He isn't much
   to look at, but he's my last admirer.

Mick Jagger's Penis Turns 69

Amorak Huey

Mick Jagger's penis is pleased to meet you.
Mick Jagger's penis is the John Lennon's penis
of penises. Also, the Steven Tyler scarf collection
of penises, the David Lee Roth midair crotch thrust,
the Gene Simmons codpiece, the Axl Rose attitude of penises.
This is a lot of pressure for a penis,
big shoes for a penis to fill. Mick Jagger's penis
doesn't ask for much, these days. Mick Jagger's penis
is strongly influenced by the blues and knows
whom this song is about. There are two versions
of Mick Jagger's penis: the one the world sees
and the one that lies awake at night
and worries it has let someone down.
Sometimes it wants to be remembered,
to leave its mark on the world, it wants
to be more than footnote, punchline, punching bag.
Sometimes it just wants to be held.
It grows weary of everything having two meanings.
If you ask Mick Jagger's penis about its dreams,
it will tell you about a certain lightning storm
over a certain lake – which means
nothing more or nothing less than what it was:
the dark water, the sky splitting open.

If You are Lucky

Michelle McGrane

If you are lucky
you will carry one night with you
for the rest of your life,
a night like no other.
You won't see it coming.

Forget the day, the year.
It will arrive uninvoked,
an astrological anomaly.

You will remember
how every cell in your body
knew him, this stranger,

how you held your breath,
the way you searched his face.
This is how such evenings begin.

And you will be real in your skin,
bone and sinew; the way you always thought
you could be. Effortlessly.
This is how you will fit together.

His parted lips between your thighs,
your half-lit nipples darkening,
the hot-breathed arrival of desire,
the frenzied coupling
as you opened soundlessly
and the world flooded into you.

In the morning, maybe,
soon after sunrise
you will walk barefoot above a waterfall in the forest,
light-headed with the smell of sex,
laughing in your déshabillé.

You will carry
the music of this memory with you;
and from time to time,
in the small, withered hours,
your body will sing its remembering.

'You come to me quiet as rain not yet fallen'

Brian Patten

You come to me quiet as rain not yet fallen
Afraid of how you might fail yourself your
dress seven summers old is kept open
in memory of sex, smells warm, of boys,
and of the once long grass.
But we are colder now; we have not
Love's first magic here. You come to me
Quiet as bulbs not yet broken
Out into sunlight.

The fear I see in your now lining face
Changes to puzzlement when my hands reach
For you as branches reach. Your dress
Does not fall easily, nor does your body
Sing of its own accord. What love added to
A common shape no longer seems a miracle.
You come to me with your age wrapped in excuses
And afraid of its silence.

Into the paradise our younger lives made of this bed and room
Has leaked the world and all its questioning
and now those shapes terrify us most
that remind us of our own. Easier now
to check longings and sentiment,
to pretend not to care overmuch,
you look out across the years, and you come to me
quiet as the last of our senses closing.

Arrival

William Carlos Williams

And yet one arrives somehow,
finds himself loosening the hooks of
her dress
in a strange bedroom –
feels the autumn
dropping its silk and linen leaves
about her ankles.
The tawdry veined body emerges
twisted upon itself
like a winter wind . . . !

Whatever Happened to Sex?

Amorak Huey

> *Maybe back in the '60s,*
> *when sex was more popular . . .*
>
> – Freshman essay

Sex lives in a bungalow in the Hollywood Hills,
comes out only for special occasions –
anniversaries, holidays, the Oscars sometimes.
Old pals like Drugs and Rock 'n' Roll stop by,
checking up, always too quick with a compliment
on how well she's holding up, you know, considering.
Sex tries hard not to whine for the good old days
or blame her agent – *She says I should be doing*
TV! Can you imagine? – but in the evenings
after her friends have gone and the lemon sun
slumps behind the orange trees
she can't help but ache to be popular again,
to feel the heat rising from flash bulbs –
that electric thrill of being wanted –
god, to be wanted once more before dark.

Acknowledgements

Adcock, Fleur: 'Madmen' from *Poems 1960–2000*, Bloodaxe, 2000, reprinted by permission of Bloodaxe Books; Agbabi, Patience: 'The Sting' from *Transformatrix,* Canongate, 2000, reprinted by permission of Canongate; Ammons, A. R.: 'Their Sex Life', from *The Really Short Poems of A. R. Ammons* by A. R. Ammons. Copyright © 1990 by A. R. Ammons. Used by permission of W. W. Norton & Company, Inc.; Armitage, Simon: 'To His Lost Lover' from *Book of Matches*, Faber, 1993, reprinted by permission of Faber & Faber; Aubury, Nic: 'Casanever' and 'The Couple Upstairs' from *Cold Soup*, Nasty Little Press, 2013, reprinted by permission of the poet; Barber, Ros: 'Ur Thurs Reidh Ansur', first published in *Stand*, 2000, reprinted by permission of the poet; Barrett, Elizabeth: 'Intimacy' from *The Bat Doctor*, Wrecking Ball Press, 2005, reprinted by permission of the poet; Bell, Jo: 'Magnets' and 'Muse', reprinted by permission of the poet; Benyon, Kaddy: 'Guacamole', reprinted by permission of the poet; Bird, Caroline: 'The Plague' from *Trouble Came to the Turnip*, Carcanet, 2006, reprinted by permission of Carcanet Press; Brackenbury, Alison: 'And', first published in *London Magazine*, reprinted by permission of the poet; Burt, Dan: 'The End of the Affair' and 'The Faithful' from *We Look Like This*, Carcanet, 2012, reprinted by permission of Carcanet Press; Catallus, Gaius Valerius: 'Carmen 16', translation by G. M. Palmer, first published by Burlesque Press, reprinted by permission of the translator; Cavafy, C. P.: 'Remember, Body . . .' and 'He Asked about the Quality' from *The Selected Poems of C. P. Cavafy,* edited and translated by Avi Sharon, Penguin Classics, 2008. Translation and editorial matter copyright © Avi Sharon, 2008; Chase, Linda: 'Young Men Dancing' from *Young Men Dancing*, Smith/Doorstep Books, 1994, reprinted by permission of Carcanet Press; Cookman, Leo: 'Haikus to Fuck to', reprinted by permission of the poet; Cope, Wendy: 'From Strugnell's Sonnets' and 'Message' from *Making Cocoa for Kingsley Amis*, Faber, 1986, reprinted by permission of Faber & Faber; Copus, Julia: 'In Defence of Adultery' from *In Defence of Adultery,* Bloodaxe, 2004, reprinted by permission of Bloodaxe Books; cummings, e. e.: 'i like my body when it is with your'. Copyright 1923, 1925, 1951, 1953 © 1991 by the Trustees for the E. E. Cummings Trust. Copyright © 1976 by George James Firmage, 'may I feel said he'. Copyright 1935 © 1963, 1991 by the Trustees for the E. E. Cummings Trust. Copyright © 1978 by George James Firmage, from *Complete Poems: 1904–1962* by E. E. Cummings, edited by George J. Firmage. Used by permission of Liveright

'Troilism' from *Mischief Night: New and Selected Poems*, Bloodaxe, 2004, reprinted by permission of Bloodaxe Books; McCauley, Amy: 'Municipal Ambition', first published by *Ink Sweat & Tears*, reprinted by permission of the poet; McGrane, Michelle: 'If You Are Lucky' from *The Suitable Girl*, Pindrop Press, 2010, reprinted by permission of the poet; McGrane, Paul: 'Benny Hill', first published in *Nutshell* and *The Delinquent*, reprinted by permission of the poet; Magennis, Nikki: 'The Walk of Shame' from *Meeting Buddha in Dumbarton*, Red Squirrel Press, 2014, reprinted by permission of the poet; Nichols, Grace: 'My Black Triangle' from *I Have Crossed an Ocean: Selected Poems*, Bloodaxe, 2010, reprinted by permission of Bloodaxe Books; Olds, Sharon: 'Topography' and 'Sex without Love' from *Selected Poems*, published by Jonathan Cape, reprinted by permission of The Random House Group; ovid: '*Amores 1.5*' from *The Erotic Poems* by Ovid, translated with an Introduction by Peter Green (Penguin Classics, 1982). Copyright © Peter Green, 1982; Don Paterson: 'Imperial' and 'Buggery' from *God's Gift to Women*, Faber, 1997, reprinted by permission of Faber & Faber; Patten, Brian: 'You come to me quiet as rain not yet fallen' from *Notes to the Hanging Man*. Copyright © Brian Patten, 1969. Reprinted by permission of the author c/o Rogers, Coleridge & White, 20 Powis Mews, London w11 1jn; Pindar, Ian: 'On the French Riviera' from *Emporium*, Carcanet, 2011, reprinted by permission of Carcanet Press; Pitt Kethley, Fiona: 'Katya is Bored', 'Chris of Dublin' and 'Jaffa Cakes' from the series *Around the World in Eighty Lays*, reprinted by permission of the poet; Rollinson, Neil: 'Like the Blowing of Birds' Eggs' and 'Ménage à Trois' from *A Spillage of Mercury*, Jonathan Cape, 1996, reprinted by permission of the poet/'Featherlite' from *Spanish Fly*, Jonathan Cape, 2001, reprinted by permission of The Random House Group; Salway, Sarah: 'Conception' and 'The Man in the Print Room' from *You Do Not Need Another Self-Help Book*, Pindrop Press, 2012, reprinted by permission of the poet; Salzman, Eva: 'An Epic in Me' and 'Can Clio Do More than Amuse?' from *Double Crossing: New and Selected Poems*, Bloodaxe, 2004, reprinted by permission of Bloodaxe Books; Sandler, Rosie: 'Found Wanting', reprinted by permission of the poet; Sansom, Peter: 'The Day He Met His Wife' from *Selected Poems*, Carcanet, 2010, reprinted by permission of Carcanet Press; Saunders, John: 'In the Victoria Hotel' from *Chance*, New Binary Press, Ireland, 2013, reprinted by permission of the poet; Schmidt, Michael: 'Wanting to Think' from *Selected Poems 1972–97*, Carcanet, 1997, reprinted by permission of Carcanet Press; Scott, Richard: 'Sandcastles', first published in *Poetry London*, reprinted by permission of the poet; Sheehan, Eileen: 'Ego' from *Song of the Midnight Fox*, Doghouse Books, 2004, reprinted by permission of Doghouse Books and the poet; Sisson, C. H.: 'I Who Am' and 'Address' from *Poems:*

Index of Poets

Index of First Lines

Index of Titles